KU-780-904

THE BATTLE
OF THE ATLANTIC

Donald Macintyre

PEN & SWORD MILITARY CLASSICS

By the same Author

U-Boat Killer
Jutland
The Kola Run
(*in collaboration with Vice-Admiral Ian Campbell*)
Narvik
The Thunder of the Guns

First published in Great Britain in 1961 by
B. T. Batsford.

Published in this format in 2006 by
Pen & Sword Military Classics
An imprint of
Pen & Sword Books Ltd
47 Church Street
Barnsley
South Yorkshire
S70 2AS

Copyright © Donald Macintyre, 1961, 2006

ISBN 1 84415 366 5

The right of Donald Macintyre to be identified as Author of this work has been
asserted by him in accordance with the Copyright, Designs and Patents Act 1988.

A CIP catalogue record for this book is
available from the British Library

All rights reserved. No part of this book may be reproduced or transmitted
in any form or by any means, electronic or mechanical including photocopying,
recording or by any information storage and retrieval system, without permission
from the Publisher in writing.

Printed and bound in England By CPI UK

Pen & Sword Books Ltd incorporates the Imprints of Pen & Sword Aviation,
Pen & Sword Maritime, Pen & Sword Military, Wharncliffe Local history,
Pen & Sword Select, Pen & Sword Military Classics and Leo Cooper.

For a complete list of Pen & Sword titles please contact
PEN & SWORD BOOKS LIMITED
47 Church Street, Barnsley, South Yorkshire, S70 2AS, England
E-mail: enquiries@pen-and-sword.co.uk
Website: www.pen-and-sword.co.uk

CONTENTS

ACKNOWLEDGMENT

This book has been written with the full co-operation of the Admiralty, which has kindly allowed the author access to Staff Histories as well as to the Reports of Proceedings of commanders of naval units which took part in the Battle of the Atlantic.

The author wishes to record his appreciation of the always willing assistance given to him by the Admiralty librarians and historians under Lieutenant-Commander Peter Kemp, the Head of the Historical Section, and, in particular, that of Commander F. Barley and Lieutenant-Commander W. Waters whose wide, detailed and exhaustive knowledge of all aspects of the history and problems of the defence of merchant shipping in two world wars has been of inestimable value in the compilation of this book.

Finally the author wishes to acknowledge his debt to Captain Stephen Roskill, whose superb official history, *The War at Sea*, must always remain an essential source for anyone writing on any aspect of naval operations of the Second World War.

Acknowledgment is due to the publishers for permission to quote from the undermentioned books:

To Cassell and Company Ltd for the quotations on pp. 12, 29 and 64 from *The Second World War* and *War Speeches* by Sir Winston Churchill; to William Clowes and Sons, Ltd for the quotation on p. 173 from *Brassey's Annual* for 1953; to the Controller of Her Majesty's Stationery Office for the quotations on pp. 111 and 196 from *The War at Sea* by Captain S. Roskill; to John Murray Publishers for the quotation on p. 140 from *The Victory at Sea* by Admiral W. S. Sims; to the Oxford University Press for the quotations on pp. 141-3 from the *History of the U.S. Navy in World War II* by Professor Morison; to George Weidenfeld and Nicolson Limited for the quotations on pp. 111, 132, 136-7, 143, 146, 193 and 195 from *The Memoirs of Admiral Dönitz*, and for the quotation on p. 145 from *Sea Wolves* by Wolfgang Frank.

The Author and Publishers also wish to thank the following for permission to reproduce the illustrations which appear in this book: The Imperial War Museum, for figs. 2, 3, 9–15, 17, 19, 26–31 and 48–54. Südd. Verlag, Munich, for figs. 5, 6, 18, 22–4, 33 and 42–5. Ullstein Bilderdienst, Berlin, for figs. 1, 7, 8, 16, 20, 21, 34–6 and 39–41.

LIST OF ILLUSTRATIONS

Figure

Introduction

THE PHRASE 'Battle of the Atlantic' was first given public expression by Sir Winston Churchill. It concentrated attention upon an aspect of naval warfare, which on account of its often hum-drum nature is apt to be looked upon as a side-show, a back-water of the main stream of naval operations, yet which is in fact the whole purpose of seapower and in which an island power must either decisively win or be driven to abject surrender.

The task of any navy in war has been accurately and simply described as 'to enable its country to use ships where and when she wants to and to prevent an enemy from using ships where and when he wants to'. For an industrialised island power such as Great Britain or Japan this resolves itself primarily into assuring the safety of the merchant ships bringing food, fuel and the raw materials without which the war cannot be carried on and the people will be starved. Japan failed in this task and long before the first atomic bomb was dropped on Hiroshima no alternative faced her but eventual unconditional surrender. Great Britain, through a failure in the years before the Second World War to understand and prepare for this primary naval task, suffered grievous loss which reduced her capacity to wage war to a critical level before the lessons of history were learnt afresh, methods applied and weapons devised to give protection to her merchant ships.

The task of ensuring the safe passage of the merchantmen, troop-ships and transports of Great Britain and her Allies was a campaign which began on the day war was declared, spread half round the world and was still being fought when Germany accepted defeat on land and surrendered. The Battle of the Atlantic was that part of this campaign which was fought out to a decisive conclusion between September 1939 and May 1943 on the convoy routes of the North Atlantic. It was a battle on which the whole outcome of the war depended. As Sir Winston Churchill has written,

> Battles might be won or lost, enterprises might succeed or miscarry, territories might be gained or quitted, but dominating all our power to carry on the war, or even keep ourselves alive, lay our mastery of the ocean routes and the free approach and entry to our ports. . . . The only thing that ever really frightened me during the war was the U-boat peril.

It was to the Atlantic that ships from the seven seas came, cargoes in their bellies, of value to hard-pressed England beyond any treasure horde of olden times. It was in the Atlantic, therefore, that the enemy had the best chance to deliver a mortal blow. Every phase of the war against Germany was dominated by the necessity to bring our laden ships safely to port and our outgoing, empty ships away. It was from overseas that the majority of the weapons, munitions and raw materials had to come, with which to re-arm ourselves. Every gallon of petrol burnt in the skies over England during the Battle of Britain came to England in ships. The tanks, guns and ammunition with which the 8th Army won the Battle of Alamein had made sea passages of many thousands of miles in the Atlantic before they went into action, as had the soldiers themselves. The Anglo-American landings in North Africa were launched from ships convoyed safely through the enemy's U-boat concentrations at the height of his Atlantic effort. The great assault on the Normandy beaches in 1944 could not have been attempted had the enemy not been first decisively beaten in the Atlantic.

It can be fairly said that it was in the Atlantic that the Allies could have been most surely defeated. It was there, instead, that the war was won.

I

The Convoy System

THAT TWICE within a single lifetime Great Britain should have been brought to within a measurable distance of defeat through assault on the sea-borne commerce without which she cannot live is a serious indictment of the ability of the controllers of her naval strategy to appreciate and draw the correct conclusions from the lessons of the past.

On the first occasion, during the First World War, it is fair to say that it was the immensity of the changes which had taken place at sea since an ocean-wide war had last been fought, owing to the introduction of steamships, that befogged strategic thought. A new and largely untried weapon, the submarine, also assisted in bringing confusion into naval counsels. It was forgotten that new weapons do not alter the basic principles of war.

These insist upon the importance of concentration and economy of force. During the centuries of almost incessant naval warfare which came to an end with the defeat of Napoleon, the application of these principles to the defence of merchant shipping had resulted in the unquestioned adoption in time of war of the convoy system. The gathering together of the season's shipping engaged in any particular trade and sailing it in an organised fleet with a naval escort enabled the maximum protection to be afforded. At the same time it enabled the available naval force to be concentrated where the enemy was bound to come if he wished to do you hurt. So obvious was this to the seamen of Nelson's day that any other system would have been unthinkable to them. Their judgment in the matter was endorsed by the Marine Insurance Underwriters who demanded War Risks Premiums a third to a half greater for independently sailed ships than for those which sailed in convoy. In 1798 the Government passed an Act giving the Admiralty power to enforce the convoy system for all ocean-going merchant ships.

Prior to this, in spite of the heavy insurance premiums demanded of independently sailing ships, or 'runners' as they were called, there were always owners who resented the restrictions and delays imposed by waiting for convoys to assemble and were prepared to take a chance. The fate of many of these ships foreshadowed in a remarkable way that of merchant vessels of the steam age in the First World War prior to the introduction of convoys. They fell easy prey to fast privateers and small warships who were always able to evade patrolling or blockading warships, just as submarines were to prove themselves able to do. On the other hand such commerce raiders avoided convoys like the plague while there were 'runners' to be found. When 'runners' vanished from the seas and it became necessary to attack convoys, squadrons of line-of-battle ships were employed with the result that if the escort knew its duty a naval action developed while the convoy escaped scot-free.

When Napoleon surrendered to the captain of the *Bellerophon* in 1815, world wars ceased for a hundred years. During that time the great change from sail to steam produced a revolution in naval thought and methods. The basic fact which had to be taken into consideration was that, though ships were no longer at the mercy of the winds, they were completely dependent upon the availability of coaling stations. The length of the voyages and the time they could remain at sea was no longer controlled by the food and water for the crew which they could stow, but by the rate of consumption of coal by their greedy boilers.

So far as merchant ships were concerned, this was no serious restriction on their movements. Their rate of coal consumption was low and it could be obtained at most ports throughout the world. In time of war the movement of warships was, on the other hand, very greatly embarrassed. Only in ports under their own flag or that of an ally could they obtain fuel. At even moderately high speed they consumed coal at a rate which seriously limited their radius of action.

For Great Britain, which had prudently established coaling

stations all over the world, this was no hardship. Indeed, so far as the Navy's function of guarding its merchant ships went, it seemed a positive advantage in that commerce raiders, handicapped as they must be by the incessant search for replenishment of their bunkers, would be hard put to it to avoid for long being brought to action by Britain's large cruiser fleet. Furthermore, while Britain maintained a Fleet equal in size to those of any two other countries, it was believed that a blockade could be established which would prevent commerce raiders in any numbers emerging on to the oceans.

This reasoning was not unsound up to this stage. Unfortunately it was applied to a desire, not unnatural to the great and prosperous Empire which had amassed vast wealth through its sea-borne commerce, to keep its ships plying freely and untrammelled. The thought of submitting to the restrictions imposed by a convoy system was repugnant to those most independent of bodies, the shipping companies. While their ships were tied up waiting for convoys to assemble, their foreign, neutral competitors might be snapping up the trade. It was the Navy's duty, they claimed, not simply to protect our shipping but to keep it moving as in peacetime.

In the search for a strategy which would achieve both these objects, the insidious suggestion was put about that by patrolling the sea-routes along which the shipping plied it could be done. It was a siren-song to all concerned. The ship-owners could pursue the policy of 'business as usual', dear to their hearts; the Government need not stock-pile food and raw materials since the ships bringing them would be arriving with the same regularity as in peacetime; the Navy would be freed of the 'defensive' tedium of convoy escort and would be able to adopt the historic role, which they believed to have been played by their forebears, of 'seeking out and destroying the enemy'.

In 1872, the Compulsory Convoy Act was repealed. Henceforth the Royal Navy's composition and its strategy were based on the principle of blockade and patrol. A new jargon grew up in which to describe the Navy's task. It was to 'secure the sea communications', 'protect the ocean highways', 'preserve the sea-routes'—all phrases which screened the fact that merchant ships would no longer receive direct protection. That the 'patrols' which were to achieve these objects would each be, in the illimitable spaces of the ocean, like a single rifleman trying to protect a caravan in the Sahara by strolling at random to and fro along the route, was ignored by those who knew the sea and left unexplained to those who did not.

So long as only surface warships had to be considered, this false, insidious doctrine would not lead to merchant ship losses on a calamitous scale. The few commerce raiders which an enemy could get away to sea must eventually be brought to book, tied to their supplies of coal as they would be, and bereft of any dockyard facilities for repair of damage. The losses until then were acceptable in pursuit of 'business as usual'.

While the new strategic thought was becoming the orthodox doctrine for naval strategists, developments were taking place which were eventually to expose it as the heresy it was. The minds of inventors had been exploring the possibility of under-water craft at intervals for three centuries. A submersible boat had been devised by an Englishman, David Bourne, in 1578, which he had later demonstrated to King James I. It was not mobile, however, and it was not until 1776 that a mobile submersible was constructed and used in war. A craft designed and built by an American, David Bushnell, was used in an attempt to sink Admiral Lord Howe's flagship by attaching a delay-action explosive charge to the ship's bottom. In 1801 the American Robert Fulton demonstrated a similar craft to Napoleon and in the war of 1812 it was used in the same way in an attempt to sink the line-of-battle ship *Ramillies,* flagship of Commodore Hardy. In 1864, during the American Civil War, came the first successful submarine attack when the Federal warship *Housatonic* was sunk in harbour by an explosive charge attached to her bottom.

These early experiments made but a momentary ripple on the calm surface of established naval thought, because the craft lacked two elements to make it effective against a reasonably alert enemy. These were an engine to drive it when totally submerged, and a self-propelled, under-water weapon. The first was to be provided by the invention of the electric motor driven by storage batteries. The second, the mobile torpedo, owes its early development to an Englishman, Robert Whitehead, working for the Austrian Government. It was not a very formidable weapon at first. By 1868 it could carry an 18-lb. explosive charge some 400 yards at 6 knots, running at a depth between five and fifteen feet. Two years later its performance had been increased to give it a range of 700 yards at 8 knots. At this stage the Austrian Government, failing to appreciate the revolutionary weapon being placed in its hands, withdrew its financial backing to the project. The British Admiralty seized the opportunity to invite Whitehead to bring his torpedoes to England and develop them under its auspices.

Thereafter the torpedo steadily gained in size, range, speed and destructive effect. When submarines became fully sea-going, the torpedo was the weapon perfectly tailored to their requirements. The threat they represented was not unappreciated by the British Government and Admiralty. So long as submarines could attack from below the surface, the only defence against them at first was high speed and a zig-zag course to make it difficult for them to achieve an attacking position and to complicate the problem of aiming their torpedoes. Merchant ships, therefore, with their slow speed were defenceless.

On the other hand the Rules of War, as laid down by The Hague Convention, denied the right of any warship to sink any unescorted merchant ship without warning, or indeed to sink any without first visiting and searching it to decide whether its cargo was contraband. Even then the crew had to be ensured a safe means of reaching land, for which purpose the ship's lifeboats were not considered sufficient. Clearly submarines, which became highly vulnerable as soon as they surfaced and could not possibly accommodate the crew of any merchant ship they decided to sink, were gravely handicapped in any action against sea-borne commerce. In fact, if they held to the Rules of War, they could not be so used.

To a generation to which the expression 'Total War' has become familiar, a faith in the acceptance of any Rules of War by any belligerent who found them operating to their serious disadvantage may seem ingenuous. The fact remains that it was believed by the British that the rule of visit and search, which operated entirely in favour of themselves, would be observed. Anything else was considered barbarous. Thus in the years before the First World War the possibility of submarines constituting a serious threat to our merchant ships was discounted. No plans or preparations were therefore made to adopt a convoy system on the outbreak of war. Furthermore so unanimous were the voices, naval and mercantile, stressing the great difficulties of introducing such a system, that, when the Germans adopted the principle of unrestricted U-boat warfare, it was not until merchant ship losses had reached a figure which spelt total defeat for Great Britain that such a system was considered.

Up to the end of 1916 the desire not to bring neutrals, particularly America, into the war against her, acted to prevent Germany from waging an altogether ruthless U-boat war. The majority of merchant ships sunk were first stopped by the U-boat on the surface. In spite of all efforts by thousands of surface anti-submarine craft, 70 airships and huge numbers of seaplanes and flying-boats 'patrolling the sea-lanes', this method had sunk 1,360 ships, while only four U-boats had been sunk by these ubiquitous patrols.

Germany's U-boat fleet had been constantly expanding since the beginning of the war. By the end of 1916 there were 100 operational U-boats. The decision was taken to throw off all restrictions on them and to gamble all on quickly starving Britain into submission. Between the 1st February, 1917, and the end of April 800 ships, totalling nearly two million tons, were sunk.

With disaster staring us in the face, the Naval Staff, presided over by Admiral Jellicoe who had been specially brought in as First Sea Lord to deal with the U-boat problem, continued to set its face against the introduction of a convoy system. Every possible objection to it, many of them based on false figures and false assumptions, was thought out by Rear-Admiral Duff who had accompanied Jellicoe from the Grand Fleet to the Admiralty to head a newly formed Anti-Submarine Division: the ports would become congested if ships of a convoy all arrived simultaneously; merchant ships had not the facilities necessary for adjustment of their speed to maintain station in convoy; the convoys themselves would constitute large and easy targets; finally there were simply not enough escorts.

This last objection was the crucial one. It was based on figures accepted by the Admiralty representing the number of inward and outward voyages to and from British ports, the fantastic number of 2,500 each way each week. The only solution, the Admiralty reported to the Government, was to intensify 'offensive' operations against the U-boats, increasing the already huge force of patrol vessels and aircraft, mining the U-boats into their bases and to build merchant ships at a rate which would outstrip the losses. It was a policy of despair, as can be shown by the figures of losses. In one week in September 1916, three U-boats, operating between Beachy Head and the Eddystone, sank 30 ships. Although 49 destroyers, 48 torpedo boats, seven Q-ships, 468 armed auxiliaries and a large number of aircraft patrolled the area and hunted the submarines, they escaped unharmed.

While the Board of Admiralty thus virtually admitted themselves beaten by the problem, although there were a number of junior officers at the Admiralty who were convinced that convoy was the solution, it fell to the French Government to be the first to insist upon a convoy system. The cross-channel coal trade was of vital importance to them. It was being decimated by the U-boats, while the colliers were sailing independently. From February 1917, at the insistence of the French, they were sailed in convoy and at once gained almost total immunity. In the North, Admiral Beatty, commanding the Grand Fleet, and responsible for the safety of the Scandinavian trade, faced by a steady 25 per cent loss rate was given grudging permission to put the merchant ships in convoy in the middle of April with a consequent startling reduction in losses to 0·24 per cent.

Nevertheless it was not these results which finally induced the Admiralty to take the great and saving decision to introduce a convoy system elsewhere. The credit must go to Lloyd George, at that time Prime Minister, and to Sir Maurice Hankey, Secretary to the War Cabinet.

The Prime Minister, faced with the clear-cut fact that a solution to the U-boat problem had to be found or the war was lost and that the responsibility for the conduct of the war was ultimately his, decided that the problem must be studied in the light of basic principles, stripped of all the technicalities with which the Admiralty shrouded it and which only an expert could disentangle. A masterly paper by Sir Maurice Hankey, based on information obtained from two comparatively junior officers in the Admiralty, Commanders K. G. B. Dewar and R. G. Henderson, set forth the arguments for and against a convoy system and included a crushing indictment of the existing system. 'How under this system', he wrote, 'we are ever to avoid losses limited only by the number of the enemy's sea-going submarines and his output of torpedoes, it is difficult to see.' In favour of the convoy system he made the penetrating comment: 'Perhaps the best commentary on the convoy system is that it is invariably adopted for our main fleet, and for our transports.'

At the same time Dewar and Henderson, incredulous of the shipping figures, had made an investigation of their own, in which they discovered that the figure 2,500 included every ship over 300 tons, whatever its employment. Thus not only coasters had been taken into account but even such craft as the Isle of Wight ferries. The figure for ocean-going merchant ships was in fact between 120 and 140.

It is not surprising that the Prime Minister, who was fortunately not above getting his information from junior officers, decided to force the Admiralty's hand. On the 25th April, 1917, he announced that he was coming to visit the Admiralty on the 30th, 'and there take peremptory action on the question of convoys'. The implied prospect of being overruled was enough for the Board. On the 26th April a Minute from Admiral Duff to the First Sea Lord revealed a remarkable overnight change of opinion: 'It seems to me evident that the time has arrived when we must be ready to introduce a comprehensive scheme of convoy at any moment.' The following day Jellicoe approved the Minute.

When Lloyd George paid his visit he 'was gratified to learn from Admiral Duff that he had completely altered his view in regard to the adoption of convoy and gathered that the First Sea Lord shared his views, at any rate to the extent of an experiment'.

So in the eleventh hour came Britain's salvation. As convoys were gradually organised, at first only for inward shipping, the first one leaving Gibraltar on the 10th May, 1917, all the jeremiads about the impossibility of keeping large bodies of merchantmen together and the vulnerability of convoys were proved false. The loss rate dropped dramatically. The U-boats concentrated their attacks on the out-ward-bound ships which were still being sailed independently along the 'patrolled routes'. That even now the virtue of convoy was not fully appreciated is shown by the complaint which followed, that the outward ships were suffering because patrol vessels had been reduced to make up convoy escorts. It was not until August 1917 that outward convoys began to run. In November they were instituted for the Mediterranean. Everywhere the story was the same. Losses in convoy were one tenth those amongst independently sailed ships.

The sorry story of British reluctance to follow the dictates of history in the matter of protection of shipping has been set out at some length, as it is essential in a study of the Battle of the Atlantic to appreciate why it took the form it did, and to answer any sug-gestions that it could have been avoided by an abandonment of the convoy system. Fortunately, in spite of a body of naval opinion which to this day questions the virtue of convoy on the grounds that a fighting force is by it condemned to a defensive role, when war came again in September 1939, the Admiralty's plans for the im-mediate institution of a convoy system were ready. Indeed the lessons learnt in 1917 were for the most part too startling, too dramatic to be overlooked or forgotten by those responsible for our defence arrangements in 1939. One aspect was however obscured from all but the most perceptive students of the history of the First World War. It must be mentioned here as this was to have serious implications when war came again.

The success achieved by the convoying of our merchantmen by warships had been clear beyond any risk of misunderstanding. On the other hand the even more remarkable success achieved by the addition of air escort to the surface escort had not. The history of the somewhat dull, prosaic work of the seaplanes and airships of the R.N.A.S. had been recorded not in the Naval Histories, but in that of the Royal Air Force which had absorbed the Royal Naval Air Service on the 1st April, 1918. There it was submerged in the much more exciting froth of the accounts of thrilling battles in the air and devastating bomber raids. Thus an astonishing fact which emerges from a close examination of the history of those times was overlooked. Of the 96 ships sunk out of the 16,000 sailed in ocean convoys and the 161 lost from the 68,000 sailed in coastal and short sea convoys, only five were so sunk when an air escort was present as well as surface escorts. This was in spite of the fact that, owing to the lack of any weapon with which to attack a submerged submarine, aircraft sank none.

These figures should be remembered when we come to study the course of the Battle of the Atlantic and the resources at the disposal of the Royal Navy during it. It had been one thing to decide the form of protection which would be given to our merchant fleet in time of war; quite another to extract from an unwilling Parliament and nation the funds to provide the warships and aircraft needed to implement it.

2

Opening Skirmishes

THE HOLOCAUST of the youth of the opposing nations in the First World War was so appalling, the exhaustion of both sides so complete, that the conception that it had been a 'war to end wars' gained a ready acceptance amongst the victors. It was inconceivable to a generation which had known the blood and mud of Flanders that war could ever again be resorted to. Thus, as so often in England's history, her Navy was allowed to dwindle. The assumption that no war need be prepared for within the next ten years was renewed from year to year. On that basis the ship-building programme for the Navy was kept down to minute proportions. The Royal Air Force was similarly starved, with only the veriest crumbs from the meagre annual estimates being allocated to Coastal Command. As the R.A.F. Official History records, 'The task of producing a fighter force capable of protecting our cities and a bomber force able to strike back at Germany had absorbed most of our energies and out-put, leaving very little over for purely maritime aircraft.' The priorities which are disclosed by this frank statement betray the lack of appreciation of this country's utter dependence on sea-borne traffic, which has repeatedly led her to the brink of defeat. But for Germany's unpreparedness at sea, the fighters and bombers might well have been immobilised for lack of petrol, every gallon of which had to come in from overseas.

The apparent completeness of the defeat of the U-boat in 1918 had led to unjustified confidence that the under-water menace to our merchant shipping had been mastered. This confidence was enhanced by the invention at the end of the war of a submarine detecting device, the ASDIC—so-called from the initials of the Allied Submarine

Detection Investigation Committee under whose auspices it was developed. In conjunction with the depth-charge, a means of detecting and destroying a submerged submarine had been at long last achieved. As the asdic remained, throughout the war, the only device by which a surface ship could detect and locate a submerged submarine, and as its composition and method of operation must be broadly understood to follow the details of anti-submarine tactics, a simplified description of it is given in the Appendix (p. 197).

This development and a strange and unjustified belief that in any future war enemy submarines would once again allow their operations to be circumscribed by adherence to the Rules of War, led to the assumption that the principal threat to our merchant shipping would come from surface raiders. As late as 1937 the Naval Staff reported that in their opinion 'the submarine would never again be able to present us with the problem we were faced with in 1917'. Consequently not only was the primary task of Coastal Command enunciated as that of reconnoitring the North Sea to watch for the break-out of surface raiders, but no provision was made for convoy escorts beyond the existing asdic-fitted force of some 150 destroyers, half of which were veterans of the First World War maintained in reserve, coastal patrol vessels and 24 sloops.

That the size of this force may be seen in proper perspective, the task which faced it may be judged by the fact that in 1939 there were 3,000 deep-sea dry cargo merchant ships and tankers and 1,000 coasters registered in Great Britain totalling 21 million tons. The average number of ships at sea on any one day was 2,500. The 150 escort destroyers and almost total absence of aircraft for escort duties can be compared with the 1918 figures of 257 warships employed solely on escort with a further 500 so employed intermittently, 190 aeroplanes, 300 seaplanes and flying boats, and 75 airships.

It was not until Hitler, in April 1939, denounced the naval treaty which had strictly limited the size of the German Navy that any thought was given to an increase in the number of our escort craft. In July and August of that year, 56 patrol vessels were ordered which were to be the first of the famous Flower-class corvettes. These were originally designed for coastal escort duties only. Though they began to come to sea in numbers in May 1940 and soon became the mainstay of our convoy escorts, it was not until they had been considerably modified for ocean work that they were reasonably efficient. Even so, their maximum speed of 16 knots was inadequate for anti-submarine work, being less than that of a surfaced German U-boat. Not until April 1942 did the first frigate of the River class, essentially designed for ocean escort work, come to sea. Jellicoe's warning, made to an unheeding Government in 1929, that 'war experience showed that the fast vessels needed for anti-submarine convoy escort cannot be hurriedly improvised' was thus substantiated.

As for air escort, at the outbreak of war Coastal Command of the R.A.F. had no aircraft designed and no aircrews trained for anti-submarine work. Such tasks were subordinate to those of reconnaissance against surface raiders.

Unfortunately the basis on which the complacency with regard to the submarine threat rested, the efficacy of the asdic, was thoroughly unsound. Peacetime exercises with it had been largely confined to hunting submarines whose initial positions were known within fairly narrow limits. Such practices were only carried out in calm or moderate weather conditions and in daylight. The anti-submarine teams engaged were highly-trained and well practised. Even so, there were at least as many unsuccessful hunts as there were 'kills'. For reasons not then understood, there were occasions when the asdic failed lamentably. Nevertheless the belief was held by all but those with considerable experience of the asdic that the submarine was mastered. It was not appreciated that the greatly increased endurance of submarines would permit them to operate far out in the Atlantic which, unlike the First World War, would mean escorting our merchant convoys for the whole of their ocean voyage. Nor was it taken into account that improved submarine capabilities and technique would enable submerged attacks to be delivered in conditions of rough weather in which the performance of the asdic was greatly reduced.

Perhaps the greatest miscalculation, caused by an incomplete study of the lessons of the First World War, was that which assumed that U-boat attacks would be confined to submerged attacks. During 1918 the U-boat commanders, one of the most successful of whom was Karl Dönitz, foiled by the surface and air escorts from attacking submerged by day, had taken to night attacks on the surface. The low silhouette of their craft enabled them to approach and deliver their attacks unseen. In an effort to combat this manœuvre, aircraft were fitted with searchlights, a development which was not resumed in the Second World War until 1942.

All this was recorded in the R.A.F. Official History. Furthermore, in a book which was published in Germany before the war and had been available to the general public, Dönitz, now commanding Hitler's U-boat fleet, had advocated the technique of the night attack on the surface.

Now the asdic suffered from certain limitations, one of which was its poor performance against small surface targets. Thus if the U-boat commanders employed the same tactics as in the First World War—and opposed by the asdic they were certain to do so—the escorts would be confined to the same means of detection as in 1918, the human eye. Thus the linch-pin of the Navy's confidence in its ability to combat the U-boat was knocked out.

So, when on the 3rd September, 1939, Britain found herself once again at war with Germany, although there was no doubt that to defend our merchant ships from attack they must be sailed in convoy —and, in fact, the first such convoy, from Gibraltar to Capetown, had sailed the day before—the means of protecting these convoys was sparse in the extreme. A great part of the force of destroyers available was absorbed in screening duties with the Fleet, escorting the Army to France and protecting the large volume of shipping always at sea off our vulnerable East Coast. Air escort was virtually non-existent. R.A.F. Coastal Command consisted of a few squadrons of twin-engined Anson aircraft, whose range was limited to 510 miles and which were almost wholly absorbed by the task of North Sea reconnaissance, and two squadrons of Sunderland flying-boats, which had a radius of 850 miles. The few remaining surface escorts took the outward-bound Atlantic convoys only as far as 12½ degrees west longitude—some 100 miles west of Ireland. Thence the merchant ships continued in company for two more days before dispersing to sail independently to their destinations. The escorts would meanwhile have met the homeward convoy which, having assembled at Halifax, Nova Scotia, would have crossed the ocean under escort of an armed merchant cruiser.

Inadequate as these measures were to prove as the war developed, they were at first, so far as ships in convoy were concerned, very successful. The German Navy, plunged into war by Hitler's policies seven years before they had expected it, was still at the beginning of its planned expansion. It possessed only 57 operational U-boats of which 30 were short-range boats suitable only for the North Sea. Of the 27 ocean-going types, 17 had sailed for the Atlantic during August. On an average, however, the number on patrol at any one time was usually about one third of the total available.

From the very start, the U-boat commanders shunned attacks on convoys so long as other targets presented themselves. Consequently by the end of 1939 they had only succeeded in sinking four ships in convoy. Convoy proved itself effective against air attack also, only eight ships being sunk by this method while in convoy. The convoy system was not, however, complete. A vestigial remnant of the old objections to it remained in the decision that ships of over 15 knots or which had a maximum speed of less than nine should be sailed independently. History at once repeated itself. From these 'runners' or 'independents' as they were now called and from unescorted groups of ships, no less than 102 ships were sunk during the same period. In achieving this the Germans had lost five U-boats to the depth charges of destroyers and three others to the mine barrage laid in the Straits of Dover.

The vulnerability of 'independents' was not the only lesson from the past painfully re-learnt in the first few months of the war. The old desire for 'offensive action' and unwarranted faith in the capabilities of the asdic had led to the formation of hunting groups. The First Lord of the Admiralty, Winston Churchill, his considerable military knowledge and experience misapplied to naval matters, penned a minute to the First Sea Lord in which he said,

Nothing can be more important in the anti-submarine war than to try to obtain an independent flotilla which could work like a cavalry division on the approaches, without worrying about the traffic or the U-boat sinkings, but could search large areas over a wide front. In this way these areas would become untenable to U-boats.

A basic error, which is to recur again and again in strategic thought on the Battle of the Atlantic, is here revealed. At nearly all stages of the Battle, the U-boat proved itself almost immune to surface or airborne search, except in the vicinity of convoys where, the area to be searched being greatly reduced, the submarine could either be kept submerged and so prevented from working its way in to the attack or, if it surfaced in order to do so, could be detected and attacked.

It is necessary to make this clear at the outset of any account of the Battle of the Atlantic as it is the root and heart of the matter. Only during brief periods when our ships and aircraft were in possession of detecting devices about which the enemy were ignorant did search and patrol have any success. The first six weeks of the war made such a period. The Germans were still unaware of the capabilities of the asdic and had not yet evolved tactics to avoid detection by patrolling anti-submarine craft. Consequently one U-boat in September and one in October 1939, failing to take the necessary evasive action on the approach of such patrols, and then unwisely betraying their position by firing torpedoes, were detected and sunk. Thereafter hunts for U-boats in the open sea were uniformly unsuccessful.

Unfortunately the British naval commands, in their laudable quest for means of offensive action against the U-boat, were slow to be convinced of the fatuity of search and patrol. Not only did the system wastefully tie up ships urgently needed for convoy escort but it was to cost us, in the first month of the war, one of our most valuable fleet units. Hunting groups had been formed, each consisting of an aircraft-carrier and a small destroyer screen. The naval aircraft, not being equipped at that time with radar, had no success whatever. On the 14th September the aircraft-carrier *Ark Royal* with one such group was narrowly missed by a U-boat's torpedoes. Three days later the *Courageous,* similarly occupied, was torpedoed and sunk by *U29* with a heavy loss of life.

The first six months of the long struggle which was to last for six years can be described as the opening skirmishes before battle was fully joined. During these skirmishes each side probed the other's defences and learnt what it was up against. The U-boat commanders learnt to respect the ability of asdic-fitted warships to detect and attack them submerged. They therefore concentrated, when possible, on unescorted independents, from which there was still a rich harvest to be reaped. They also discovered, to their considerable dismay, that the torpedoes with which they were armed were unreliable, both the depth-keeping mechanism and the firing system of the magnetic pistols in the warheads being liable to failure. The Allies, on the other hand, reached a clearer understanding of the limitations of the asdic. It was realised that escorts in greater and greater numbers were needed. Unfortunately belief in the efficacy of patrol and search lingered on. Much of the asdic-fitting effort was put into equipping trawlers, drifters and coastal forces which in the event were not to account for more than six German and Italian U-boats in the entire course of the war. Losses of ships in convoy, at first almost negligible, rose sharply in February 1940 because too many escort vessels were being used to sweep the empty ocean wastes while convoys were left with perhaps a single destroyer or sloop as escort. This was in spite of the recommendations of a committee under Vice-Admiral Sir T. H. Binney which sat to review the problem. 'The best place for anti-submarine vessels', they said, 'is in company with a convoy rather than dispersed in hunting units.' During this opening phase the German U-boat commanders, who had begun the war restricted by Hitler's orders to wage war in accordance with The Hague Convention, were gradually given greater freedom in the direction of unrestricted submarine warfare.

On the first day of the war the liner *Athenia* was sunk by torpedo without warning but this was in flagrant disobedience of orders. As soon as Hitler came to realise that Britain would under no circumstances agree to a compromise peace, however, a series of edicts was issued which steadily whittled away all restrictions. On the 23rd September, 1939, it was decreed that any merchant ships making use of radio on being stopped by a U-boat should be sunk or taken in prize. On the 17th October the U-boat commanders were given permission 'to attack without warning all ships identified as hostile', with the exception of liners. A month later even this last restriction was removed.

Meanwhile the zone in which all ships steaming without lights were liable to attack without warning was gradually extended farther out into the Atlantic. By the end of the year, the U-boat campaign against Allied shipping had assumed the shape which it was to retain for the rest of the war. Any Allied merchant ship could be sunk at sight without warning, though it was not until August 1940 that Hitler announced that neutrals would be treated in the same way. This first, skirmishing period came to an end in March 1940. Hitler was planning his invasion of Norway. Every available U-boat was required to operate against the warships of the British Home Fleet which were expected to counter-attack the invading force.

While the opposing forces in the U-boat war had been seeking to get their opponents' measure, another form of attack on our Atlantic shipping had similarly been given its first test. Towards the end of August 1939 the pocket-battleships *Admiral Graf Spee* and *Deutschland* had left their home ports and, circling far to the north, had made their way unseen to waiting positions in unfrequented parts of the ocean. While Hitler continued to hope that Britain and France would make peace, the two ships were kept inactive; but on the 26th September they received orders to begin operations.

Graf Spee's area was in the South Atlantic, off the Cape of Good Hope and in the Indian Ocean. All ships in those seas were still being sailed independently. Consequently nine of them, totalling 50,000 tons, were intercepted and sunk before the pocket-battleship was brought to book off the River Plate in December. It was a small achievement when compared with those of the U-boats in the same period; but it had had the effect of tying no less than 15 British and French cruisers, three aircraft-carriers and three battle cruisers to fruitless searches in which they vainly steamed many thousands of miles and burnt away great quantities of oil fuel. *Deutschland* was given the North Atlantic for her operational area. Here the introduction of the convoy system had swept the shipping routes almost bare. During two months of disconsolate roving of a rough and empty ocean she found only two independently sailing merchantmen before being recalled to Germany.

So ended the first operation by German surface warships to attack our shipping in the Atlantic. It had been Admiralty opinion that they constituted the greatest menace which we had to fear. But, although such excursions were a considerable potential threat capable of causing a painful dislocation of sea traffic while such powerful ships were at large, they proved in fact to be far less effective than the U-boat operations. In the course of the war, indeed, surface raiders accounted for less than one-twentieth of our losses and these were almost exclusively from independently routed ships.

There were two other types of attack on our merchant shipping —mine-laying and air attack. The former which had started on the first day of war, was to take a considerable toll in ships and was to require much effort, ingenuity and courage to defeat. It was, how-ever, mainly confined to the waters round our coasts and so cannot properly be included in an account of the Battle of the Atlantic. Air attack, until Germany came into possession of air bases in France in the summer of 1940, was similarly limited to our coastal waters, principally to ships on the East Coast and in the convoys to and from Norway. It is therefore not really part of our story at this stage.

So, while on land with the end of the bitter winter 1939-40 and the arrival of spring there came the distant rumble of the *blitzkrieg* being prepared, at sea there was a lull. The two opponents in the ring had gone to their respective corners to recuperate for the rounds which were to follow. Each was not unsatisfied with his performance so far. Each expected to come out for the next round stronger than before.

But before the bell rang again conditions had so altered that one of them was to find himself fighting under disadvantages he had never visualised. The loss or damage to a great many British destroyers during the Norwegian campaign and the evacuation of the Army from Dunkirk greatly reduced the forces available for convoy escort, a shortage made worse by the decision to retain destroyers on our coasts to guard against invasion. More serious still was the establishment of air and submarine bases by the Germans along the French Atlantic coast. There was no longer any room for easy complacency about the mortal threat to Britain's shipping and supplies on which her continuance in the war and her very life depended.

In July 1940 the first Atlantic U-boat base came into operation at Lorient on the Bay of Biscay coast. At once the submarines' route to their patrol area was reduced by 450 miles. Not only could they remain longer on patrol but a greater proportion of the total number available could be kept in action. In spite of having lost 25 boats since the beginning of the war, replacements, which were beginning to come forward at an ever increasing pace, had kept this total up to 51. Furthermore, the U-boat commanders, profiting from experience in encounters with asdic-fitted ships, had come to realise that the tactics of 1918—night attack on the surface—not only gave them the speed to enable them to return to the attack again and again, but brought them almost complete immunity from detection.

Submerged, the U-boat was forced, by the need to conserve her batteries, to creep along at 3 or 4 knots. On the surface 18 knots were available, a speed greater than that of some of the escorts. Although independents or stragglers from convoys were naturally the preferred victims, lightly defended convoys were also attacked. It was found that the risk in doing so was small. With its low silhouette, the U-boat's sinister shape could not be picked out against the dark background of the night sea by look-outs high up on the bridges of destroyers and sloops. Their victims, on the other hand, and the escorts whom they must avoid, stood out stark against the lighter background of the sky.

It was at this very time that escorts were so scarce that large convoys were sailing under protection of a single destroyer or sloop. Coastal Command's ability to help was similarly cut to the bone owing to the priority given to scouting in the North Sea, which was to give early warning of the sailing of any invasion fleet. The Air Officer Commander-in-Chief, Air Marshal Sir F. W. Bowhill, pressed constantly for an increase in the strength of his Command and in particular for an allocation of the long-range, four-engine aircraft now becoming available. Ill-founded belief in the efficacy of strategic bombing led to priority being given to Bomber Command. A further handicap to the airmen of Coastal Command was the absence of an efficient weapon with which to attack U-boats. The anti-submarine bomb with which they were armed, which had a very short delay-action fuse, depended for success on a direct hit on the submarine still surfaced or a very near miss on one awash. Only a criminally unalert U-boat crew were likely to present themselves as such a target.

The ineffectiveness of these bombs was brought clearly home by the accounts given by several of our own submarines which were attacked in error with them. Some sort of airborne depth-charge was obviously called for. Experiments to produce one had been taking place, giving good promise of success, when in April 1940 the Air Ministry decided to abandon the project. It was only the impassioned pleas of Air Marshal Bowhill to have the trials resumed, and his unremitting personal efforts, which overcame the results of this disastrous decision. A few airborne depth-charges were issued to Coastal Command aircraft in the summer of 1940. In August of that year the first successful attack by aircraft of Coastal Command was achieved with one of these weapons when *U51* was seriously damaged. It was not until the following year, however, that these depth-charges were perfected and produced in sufficient numbers for them to become the standard weapon of naval and R.A.F. anti-submarine aircraft.

Under these conditions it is easy to understand why the summer of 1940 came to be called by the U-boat commanders 'The Happy Time'. In the five months, June to October, 1940, 274 ships, a total of 1,395,000 tons, were sunk at the cost of no more than six U-boats, only two of which were lost as a result of attacking merchant ships.

Encouraged by the easy pickings apparently to be found, Mussolini's submarines hastened like vultures to the scene of a killing. By November 1940, 26 were operating in the Atlantic; but they proved quite unequal to the task and proved more a hindrance than a help to Admiral Dönitz. Hitler too was encouraged by the resounding successes of his U-boat commanders, particularly as the claims of many of them were inevitably exaggerated, to cast away the last restriction upon a total blockade of the British Isles. On the 17th August he warned neutral shipping that they would be sunk at sight without warning. Victory at sea and, consequently, victory everywhere seemed in sight to the Germans.

Had the story ended here it would indeed have constituted an overwhelming victory for the U-boats. In the next chapter a description of the decimation of certain Atlantic convoys at this time will show the helplessness of the convoy escorts to defend their charges with the means available to them. But the long story of the Battle of the Atlantic had barely begun. The fight was to sway back and forth several times before a decision was reached.

Before we go on to watch it, a new participant in the battle must be recorded. At an aerodrome, near Bordeaux, the first squadron of Focke-Wulf 'Kondor' four-engined, long-range aircraft had established itself in August. Adapted from a civil air-liner, the F.-W. 200, which was its short title, had a range far in excess of anything available to Coastal Command. Reconnoitring far out into the Atlantic, its primary task was to report the positions of convoys and to act as a radio beacon for U-boats in the vicinity. This task accomplished, it was free to expend its bomb-load on the almost defenceless merchant ships, opposed only by the quite inadequate and unsuitable armament of the few escorts spread at wide intervals round the convoys. Here was another opponent against whom, as yet, the convoys were helpless. In the first two months of its operations the F.-W. 200 sank 30 merchant ships totalling 110,000 tons. The outlook was indeed one of unrelieved gloom for the crews of the merchant ships, whose chances of being sunk were high and of being rescued thereafter were all too low. For the escorts, who were forced to watch in impotent despair their convoys being decimated, it was hardly less daunting. Let us now make the North Atlantic passage with some of the convoys at sea in the late summer of 1940.

3

'The Happy Time' of the U-Boats

BY THE LATE SUMMER OF 1940, all ships homeward bound across the Atlantic, whose speeds were less than 15 knots, were making the journey in convoys, fast or slow. The fast convoys, comprising ships with a maximum speed between 9 and 14·9 knots, assembled at Halifax, Nova Scotia. The slow convoys, in which the lower speed limit was 7½ knots, began their voyage at Sydney, Cape Breton. The former were designated HX, the latter SC.

The SC convoys had been initiated at the end of July 1940 and had been intended to run only during the summer months, but necessity compelled their continuance through the savage storms of the North Atlantic winter. The fine seamanship of their masters enabled large bodies of the slow, under-powered and heavily-laden ships to be kept together in spite of tempests and enemy attack. Thus the SC convoys continued to run throughout the war and played a vital part in the eventual defeat of the U-boats. Outward bound convoys at this time were differentiated by their ports of origin, not by their speed. OA convoys were those gathered together from ports on the East Coast of Britain. OB convoys comprised ships from Liverpool, the Clyde, South Wales and Belfast.

U-boats were not yet ranging across the Atlantic so these convoys were dispersed on crossing the fifteenth west meridian, their escorts then meeting homeward convoys which up to this point had sailed with an escort of an armed merchant cruiser or a solitary sloop. Little or no protection against U-boat attack was thus provided west of 15 degrees west. As the number of escorts gradually increased and the density and efficiency of the air patrols of Coastal Command improved, so the U-boats shifted their operations westward. In this they were aided by the possession of bases on the west coast of France. One of these westward extensions of activity had occurred during August and September 1940. Heavy losses were inflicted amongst ships after they had been dispersed from outward-bound convoys and on homeward-bound convoys before their local escort had joined. The dispersal point was shifted to 17 degrees west. This was still not far enough out, but was the limit imposed by the shortage of escorts.

It was not only amongst unescorted ships that the U-boats were now achieving success. Appreciating by now that the asdic had greatly reduced a submarine's immunity when submerged, and harassed by the still sparse air patrols maintained in the vicinity of convoys by day, the U-boat commanders had reverted to the methods of the First World War which had been employed by Karl Dönitz, now chief of the U-boat arm. Approaching convoys by night on the surface, they found that they could pass quite close to the escorts and yet remain undetected. There were several reasons why they were able to do so. Look-outs in the escorts were for the most part newly joined men with meagre experience of the sea. There had been little or no time to train them in the art of seeing at night or the proper use of binoculars, without which they were almost useless at night.

Their look-out stations were far from being sheltered. Wind whipping across their faces caused their eyes to stream; spray spattering on their binoculars constantly fogged the lenses. Above all, they were necessarily stationed high up, around the bridge, so that the low shape of a U-boat had to be detected against the darkness of the water, whereas from a submarine a surface ship stood out stark against the lightness of the sky.

While visual detection of a U-boat was thus unlikely, the asdic was proving equally ineffective against a surfaced U-boat. The sound beam became diffused near the surface and failed to send back a recognisable echo. Furthermore a mistaken idea had gained currency at this time that U-boats were using the asdic transmissions of escorts

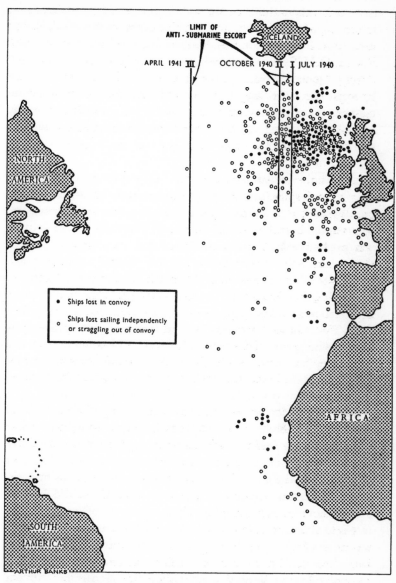

4 *The U-boats spread westwards in search of unescorted shipping*
June 1940 to April 1941

to detect the convoys. In consequence escorts were enjoined not to transmit on their asdics by night until an attack had been made on the convoy. In fact, the propeller noises of the ships could be heard in hydrophones over considerable distances which was quite enough to lead the U-boats to their prey.

For these several reasons, the immunity of U-boats from detection by night was such that the bolder and more skilful of their commanders were penetrating to the middle of the convoys before loosing their torpedoes at point-blank range. No wonder this was known as 'The Happy Time'!

Such was the situation in October 1940 when two convoys of heavily laden ships for Britain set out to cross the Atlantic. The first to sail was SC7 on the 5th of that month, 35 slow and elderly ships whose speed in convoy would not exceed 7 knots unless the weather was exceptionally favourable. Nevertheless they and the cargoes they carried were of inestimable value to Britain, still desperately striving to make up the losses suffered at Dunkirk. The formation in which convoys sailed, once they were out in the ocean, was a broad-fronted rectangle. Thus a convoy of 35 ships would be formed up in five columns of four ships and three columns of five ships each, the longer column being in the centre. The columns would be five cables (half a mile) apart, the ships in column three cables (600 yards) apart. Allowing for ships not being always well closed up, the convoy thus covered a sea area of some five square miles.

Such a formation was necessary for several reasons. Long columns invariably become strung out. Whereas a column of five ships would probably be one and a half miles long, 15 ships would rarely be less than six or seven. Thus the broad-fronted formation was more compact from the point of view of escorting, while signals from the Commodore, leading one of the centre columns, could be seen simultaneously from all ships. Furthermore, it offered a smaller target to submarines which normally attacked from the flank. Also the range of a torpedo being limited, ships in the middle columns were often immune from torpedoes fired from outside the screen of escorts. Convoys were manœuvred by flag signals by day and coloured lights by night. They could alter course by wheeling, the normal, though protracted method of changing direction; or they could be ordered, in an emergency, to turn 45 degrees to port or starboard, all ships turning together. Progress would then be in echelon, a formation which could not long be maintained without confusion arising.

The ocean escort for SC7 was the little sloop *Scarborough*, a lightly-armed warship designed for peacetime police work on distant foreign stations. In command of her was Commander N. V. Dickinson. *Scarborough* had reached Sydney a few days earlier, having carried on independently across the Atlantic after the dispersal of the outward OB216 at 17 degrees west on the 23rd September. She brought with her a tale of havoc being wrought by the U-boats in the North Channel, between Iceland and Scotland. Out of a total of 19 ships, six had been sunk between nightfall and midnight of the 20th. No trace of the submarines had been picked up by the escort. The convoy was left in peace, thereafter, the U-boats having fatter prey to seek in homeward-bound convoys. On the day before the convoy dispersed a solitary home-bound merchant was spoken. She was the *Pacific Grove*, which had broken away from convoy HX72 during an attack the previous night when six ships had been torpedoed.

A deep sense of the futility of their efforts in the face of their skil-ful and elusive tormentors could not but weigh on the minds of Dickinson and his men. Now this one little sloop was the sole defence of 34 ships until a local escort should meet them in the Western Approaches.

There was little leisure for the senior officer of the escort to ponder what might be in store. A southerly gale which sprang up on the fourth day after sailing put the convoy in disarray. During the night four Great Lakes steamers, not designed for the Atlantic rollers, lost touch and did not rejoin. Three of them were to suffer the usual fate of stragglers, being sunk by U-boats. For the next four days a speed of little better than 6 knots was the best that could be maintained.

On the 16th October, as dusk was falling, two more escorts met the convoy—unusually far west, 21° 30'. They were the *Fowey*, a sister ship of the *Scarborough*, and the *Bluebell*, one of the new

Flower-class corvettes which were now beginning to come to sea. They were commanded by Merchant Navy officers belonging to the Royal Naval Reserve, fine professional seamen who were to form the backbone of the Atlantic escorts for the rest of the war; but that at this stage of the war they and their young R.N.V.R. officers and largely conscript seaman ratings were untrained for and inexperienced in anti-submarine warfare would not be denied. These three ships, none of which had worked together before, and amongst which there was no common tactical doctrine or prepared plan of action in case of an attack, took station round the convoy, *Scarborough* on the port bow, *Fowey* to starboard and *Bluebell* astern. Visual communication between them was impossible by night. The radio link was tenuous and unreliable. The distance between them, some six miles, was more than enough for a surfaced U-boat to slink through undetected even though a full moon was shining down from a clear sky on a smooth, silver sea.

It was a peaceful enough scene to the casual observer. Nevertheless it was fraught with hidden menace. Away on the port side of the convoy, whence the serried array of black hulls stood out against the moonlight, Korvetten-Kapitän Hans Rösing, from the conning tower of *U48*, gazed through his excellent Zeiss binoculars. The course and speed of the convoy were estimated. Then to U-boat headquarters flashed the radio message giving this information. The response was soon chirruping in the earphones of *U48*'s radio operator as orders went out to six other boats, *U100, 28, 123, 101, 99* and *46*, on a patrol line to the east and north of Rockall, the little upthrust of bare seagull-haunted rock in the Atlantic lying between the thirteenth and fourteenth meridians. They were to make for the route reported by *U48* and co-operate with her. The fat, easy target in his binoculars was too tempting to Rösing to permit him to wait passively for his colleagues to join him. At daylight air patrols might be over, forcing him to submerge and perhaps lose touch. The opportunity might be missed. A curt order to the helmsman and *U48* turned in to the attack. Just before 4 a.m. a salvo of torpedoes sped away towards the unsuspecting convoy.

Lieutenant-Commander Robert Aubrey, commanding the *Fowey*, stationed on the up-moon starboard side could be fairly sure when two distant explosions thudded under his feet and a distress rocket soared up from the convoy, that the attack must have come from the far side. He at once took his ship across to join the *Scarborough*. Together the two ships swept the area on the port side with their asdics, quartering the sea for some time but to no avail. Meanwhile Lieutenant-Commander R. E. Sherwood, R.N.R., of the *Bluebell*, had taken his ship to stand by the two torpedoed ships and eventually picked up the crews from their boats.

The convoy Commodore, Vice-Admiral L. D. Mackinnon, his broad pendant in the freighter *Assyrian*, had at once ordered an emergency turn to starboard, away from the direction of the attack. Together the 30 remaining ships had swung 45 degrees and steered thus in echelon until clear of the danger area before resuming their normal formation. With the escorts all occupied elsewhere, the convoy was now bereft of all protection. At daylight the *Scarborough* rejoined, having left *Fowey* to continue the hunt for the U-boat; but she had barely regained her station when from a Sunderland flying-boat on patrol came a signal that a U-boat had been sighted and attacked just beyond the horizon on the port quarter of the convoy. Dickinson immediately left to search for and attack it. So once again the 30 ships were left to chug slowly on unescorted. It was fortunate that *U48*, having been forced to dive by *Scarborough* and *Fowey* and later again put down by the Sunderland, had lost touch with the convoy.

Dickinson's zeal to hit back at the U-boats, and an over-estimate of the chances of a single ship being able to run down even a fairly recently located submarine, was to keep him vainly searching for more than 24 hours in the area reported by the Sunderland. By the time he decided to rejoin the convoy on the next day he had dropped so far astern that his maximum speed of 14 knots never enabled him to do so. Thus losing sight of the primary object of an escort, 'the safe and timely arrival of the convoy', he was to play no active part in the events which were to follow.

When Aubrey realised the situation he at once gave up his hunt for *U48* and took the *Fowey* hurrying after the convoy which he joined that afternoon, the 17th October. When *Bluebell* also rejoined soon after dark he stationed her on the port side, while he again took up station to starboard. Two further escorts were on their way, the sloop *Leith* and the corvette *Heartsease*; but even when they arrived the escort would be sparse in the extreme. In the meantime *U48*'s loss of contact had left the German headquarters uncertain of SC7's position and route.

Another boat, *U38*, which had also reported the convoy, had given a position considerably farther to the north. Unable to decide which of the two U-boats was in error, the U-boat Command ordered a patrol line to be established, by daylight on the 18th, just to the eastward of Rockall, at a longitude which it was estimated the convoy would reach in daylight that day. This would increase the chances of interception.

While the six submarines were moving to their new positions, however, the convoy was again located. *U38* had passed the daylight hours of the 17th in hurrying, on the surface, in a wide curve beyond the horizon, to attain an attacking position by nightfall. Soon after midnight she was in position on the dark side of the convoy which was clearly silhouetted against the moonlight. Only the single little corvette *Bluebell* barred her way. Easily evading detection, *U38* moved in. Shortly after 1 a.m. on the 18th a salvo of torpedoes was fired. Kapitän-Leutnant Liebe, captain of *U38*, was unlucky and unskilful. From this first salvo of torpedoes only one achieved a hit and this was on the freighter *Carsbreck,* third ship in the port column of the convoy. With a cargo of timber she was not easy to sink. Though she was brought to a standstill she remained afloat. The *Fowey* was at once taken to join *Bluebell* in a search for the U-boat on the port side of the convoy, but without result. Neither of these ships could do more than 14 knots, less than the U-boat's top speed on the surface, so that, unless the submarine could be forced to submerge, the chances of catching her were slim.

At this moment there came a welcome reinforcement, though still a meagre one, as the sloop *Leith* (Commander R. C. Allen, R.N.) and the corvette *Heartsease* (Lieutenant-Commander E. J. R. North, R.N.R.) arrived on the scene. As senior officer of the escort, Allen now ordered *Fowey* back to the convoy while he himself with the two corvettes searched the area astern of the convoy. There he came across the damaged *Carsbreck*. Some of her crew had taken to the boats, but the master was still aboard with others. Learning that the ship was not likely to founder and could steam at 6 knots, Allen left *Heartsease* to pick up the men in the lifeboat and escort the *Carsbreck*. He then set course to rejoin the convoy with the *Bluebell*.

All these movements had left the convoy without any close escort until *Fowey* rejoined. In the meantime *U38* had been left undisturbed to reload her tubes and come in again to the attack. Soon after 1.30 a.m. Liebe again fired a salvo. He was again unsuccessful. Admiral Mackinnon, from the bridge of the *Assyrian,* saw the track of a torpedo as it streaked across from port to starboard close ahead of his flagship. He at once switched on the green light signals ordering an emergency turn of 45 degrees to starboard. No ship in the convoy was hit. The convoy was then ordered back to its original course.

There were no further alarms that night and at daylight *Leith* and *Bluebell* rejoined as escort. During the day there was a grim sign of the enemy's activities as rafts with men clinging to them were sighted near the convoy's route. From the rafts the master and crew of 18 of the Estonian steamer *Nora* were rescued by the *Leith*. The *Nora* had been sunk five days earlier. Meanwhile, as the convoy ploughed slowly on, a deadly ambush was being prepared for it. On completion of his attack, Liebe had signalled the position, course and speed of the convoy to U-boat Headquarters. By noon on the 18th, the U-boat patrol line had sighted nothing. From *U38*'s report it seemed that the convoy might pass too far to the north for the others to intercept it. Headquarters decided to rely upon *U38*'s position and fresh instructions were sent out.

Amongst the pack of wolves which were thus closing on SC7 were two of the most successful of the U-boat commanders of that time. Commanding *U100* was Joachim Schepke whose record of tonnage sunk was only exceeded by Günther Prien, destroyer of the *Royal Oak* in Scapa Flow, and by Otto Kretschmer whose *U99* was now in the same pack. The last of these, contemptuous of the opposition he had so far encountered, planned to take his boat in amongst the columns of the convoy where he could pick his targets at point-blank range. As the sun was sinking low over the sea, ruffled only by a light breeze from the south-east, the U-boats gathered just beyond the horizon, out of sight. To the north of him, Kretschmer could see the conning-tower of *U101*. A light winked from her. It was the long awaited message 'Enemy in sight to port'. Soon afterwards the masts and funnels of a warship came into sight, then a cloud of smoke and finally the forest of masts of the convoy.

All unaware of the ambush waiting ahead, the convoy settled down for the night. Ahead of it the *Leith* weaved to and fro across the front. On the starboard bow was the *Bluebell*. At dusk the *Fowey* had been ordered to sweep for five miles astern to shake off any shadowers before resuming her station on the convoy's port side. As darkness fell, the Commodore altered the convoy's course 40 degrees to starboard which it was hoped might be unobserved by any U-boat in the vicinity. Nothing could save it from its fate, however. At 8.15 the first explosion was heard as a torpedo blew a hole in the Swedish ship *Convallaria,* second ship of the second column in from the port side. That side of the convoy was devoid of any escort as the *Fowey* had not yet returned from her abortive sweep astern. Commander Allen therefore took the *Leith* on a search in that direction, continuing outwards for ten minutes, firing starshells.

Nothing was sighted. *Leith* then turned back to comb the area astern of the convoy and round the torpedoed ship. There the *Fowey*, which had picked up the crew of the *Convallaria,* was met and in company the two ships searched vainly up the convoy wake. Meanwhile the convoy had once again been left with only the *Bluebell* as close escort. The wolves closed in. Soon after 10 p.m. a series of explosions told the tale of destruction. The log-book of *U99* gives an impression of the ease with which it was achieved.

18th October. 9.24 p.m. Exchange recognition signals with *U123.* Convoy again in sight. I am ahead of it, so allow my boat to drop back, avoiding leading destroyers. Destroyers are constantly firing starshells.* From outside, I attack the right flank of the first formation.

10.02 p.m. Weather, visibility moderate, bright moonlight. Fire bow torpedo by director. Miss.

* No doubt, unable to believe that convoy escorts could be as weak as, in fact, they were at this time, the numbers present are exaggerated and the slow sloops and corvettes are always called destroyers.

10.06 p.m. Fire stern tube by director. At 700 metres, hit forward of amidships. Vessel of some 6,500 tons sinks within 20 seconds. *I now proceed head-on into the convoy.*

10.30 p.m. Fire bow tube by director. Miss because of error in calculation of gyro-angle. I therefore decide to fire rest of torpedoes without director, especially as the installation has still not been accepted and adjusted by the Torpedo Testing Department. Boat is soon sighted by a ship which fires a white star and turns towards us at full speed continuing even after we alter course.

I have to make off with engines all out. Eventually the ship turns off, fires one of her guns and again takes her place in the convoy.

11.30 p.m. Fire bow torpedo at a large freighter. As the ship turns towards us, the torpedo passes ahead of her and hits an even larger ship after a run of 1,740 metres. This ship of 7,000 tons is hit abreast the foremast and the bow quickly sinks below the surface, as two holds are apparently flooded.

11.55 p.m. Fire a bow torpedo at a large freighter of 6,000 tons at a range of 750 metres. Hit abreast foremast. Immediately after the torpedo explosion there is another explosion, with a high column of flame from bow to bridge. Smoke rises 200 metres. Bow apparently shattered. Ship continues to burn with green flame.

19th October. 12.15 a.m. Three destroyers approach the ship and search area in line abreast. I make off at full speed to the south-west and again make contact with the convoy. Torpedoes from other boats are constantly heard exploding. The destroyers do not know how to help and occupy themselves by constantly firing starshells which are of little effect in the bright moonlight. I now start attacking the convoy from astern.

And so it went on. At 1.38 and 1.55 Kretschmer torpedoed two ships which both sank, the latter in 40 seconds. Two shots at another ship missed but a third struck forward of the ship's bridge, sinking her. Just before 4 a.m. *U99*'s last torpedo hit but failed to sink another ship from the convoy. By this time all cohesion had been lost and Kretschmer was able to stand by to see if his victim would sink, before bringing his gun into action to finish her off. Before he could do so another of the pack, *U123*, opened fire on the helpless merchantman. Some of the shells falling close to *U99*—'so that I have to leave the area quickly'—Kretschmer set course for his base at Lorient, after a night of unprecedented destruction which put his record far above that of his nearest competitor.

In the convoy it had been an appalling night. As ship after ship went down or hauled out and lay slowly sinking, torpedo tracks real and imaginary set the survivors jinking this way and that to avoid them. The risk of collision was added to that from the enemy. The ships opened the distance from their neighbours more and more until all formation and order was dissolved. By daylight the convoy was virtually scattered.

For the escorts it had been a night of shame and frustration as their vain efforts to get to grips with their elusive opponents were repeatedly interrupted by the necessity to rescue the crews of sunken ships. While the *Leith* was searching up the wake of the convoy with the *Fowey*, explosions were heard in the convoy. Soon a derelict ship was sighted, the freighter *Shekatika* from which Aubrey took off the crew before hurrying on towards the convoy. Then he came across a pathetic jumble of lifeboats and drifting wreckage from which he rescued the crew of the Dutch *Boekolo*, whose master said his ship had been sunk while stopped, picking up survivors from another ship, the *Beatus*. The *Leith* meanwhile had pressed on and had come up with a group of four ships lying crippled and sinking close to one another—*Empire Miniver, Gunborg, Niritos* and *Beatus*—with the *Bluebell* standing by them.

At this moment there came the first—and only—sight of the enemy, as a submarine was sighted ahead of the *Leith* steering away on a similar course. Allen set off at full speed, illuminating his quarry with starshells while calling *Bluebell* to join him. Though the U-boat had the legs of her pursuers, her captain was bluffed into submerging. It should have been the end of her. As *Leith*'s asdic team went into operation, contact was gained. But *Leith*, like most of the ships which at this time were on escort duty, had old, out-dated equipment and a crew sorely lacking practice in the use of it. Before an effective attack could be delivered the U-boat had given her the slip. The hunt could not be long protracted. The sea was littered with sinking ships, lifeboats and rafts. A tanker had been seen to blow up on the horizon.

Sending *Bluebell* to stand by the four crippled ships which were seen to be still afloat, Allen once more set off at 11.50 at full speed to rejoin his defenceless convoy. Half an hour later he sighted the

Fowey which had just embarked the survivors from *Shekatika* and *Boekolo*. *Fowey* was ordered to join and to get back to the convoy as fast as possible. Then yet another solitary ship was sighted. She was the *Blairspey,* another lumber ship, which had been torpedoed but was able to proceed at slow speed. She had, perforce, to be left to make the best of her way to port alone, and in fact, did so unmolested further. The disastrous count was not yet complete. Hurrying on down the track of the convoy, Allen came across another sinking ship surrounded by wreckage. It was the *Assyrian,* the flagship of the Commodore, which had been torpedoed soon after midnight at the same time as the Dutch freighter *Soesterborg,* and the *Empire Brigade*. Crews from all three including Admiral Mackinnon, the much-tried Commodore, were taken on board before the *Leith* began a vain effort for the rest of the night to round up the scattered survivors of the convoy. Dawn revealed an empty sea to the dismayed escort commander.

Aubrey had had somewhat better luck. At daybreak eight ships were in sight and he soon had them gathered together with the master of one of them, the *Somersby,* appointed as Commodore. As the day wore on, the fair weather broke. The night settled down in pelting rain, reducing visibility to a few hundred yards. The little convoy again became scattered; at daylight Aubrey found that the ship with which he had kept contact was the only one in sight.

By then, however, they were well into the North Channel where the U-boats forebore to follow them. A fresh target had been located for those with any torpedoes remaining. Shaken and tired by their ordeal, the remnants of SC7 made their way individually to port, while the escorts returned sorrowfully to their base with their crowd of survivors from sunken ships.* The disastrous count of 20 ships sunk and two more damaged, out of 34 which had started, was enough to mark October 1940 as one of the black months of the war at sea. But even as the surviving ships were entering the North Channel another convoy was suffering a similar fate.

* Two of the escort commanders, Aubrey of the *Fowey* and Sherwood of the *Bluebell* were to profit from their harsh experience to become veterans of the Battle of the Atlantic and to have their revenge on the U-boats. Aubrey was to command a ship in the famous group of U-boat killers led by Captain 'Johnny' Walker. Sherwood was to command the escort of a convoy in May 1943 the fight round which was to mark the turning point of the Battle of the Atlantic.

The fast convoy HX79 had left Halifax some days after SC7 had set out from Sydney. By the 18th October it was two days' steaming behind SC7 and making for the North Channel. It had an escort of two armed merchant cruisers, *Montclare* and *Alaunia,* and as yet no anti-submarine defence, when it was sighted and reported by Günther Prien whose boat, *U47,* having expended its torpedoes in previous attacks, had been retained at sea to send weather reports to head-quarters. *U47* was instructed to shadow the convoy and 'home' all other boats in the area to it, including those which had been attacking SC7 and still had any torpedoes remaining.

During the 18th an escort of ostensibly considerable strength had met HX79. The senior officer was Lieutenant-Commander A. B. Russell, R.N., commanding the destroyer *Whitehall*. In addition there were the minesweeper *Jason,* the corvettes *Hibiscus, Heliotrope, Coreopsis* and *Arabis,* the destroyer *Sturdy* and three trawlers, *Lady Elsa, Black Fly* and *Angle*. On paper a formidable force; but the ships of which it was composed had been got together at random; the Flower-class corvettes were newly commissioned and mostly straight from the shipyards which were now turning them out in a steady stream. Their crews lacked training and experience. None of the commanding officers of the ships of the escort had had any opportunity of meeting to discuss and determine a common plan in the event of an attack. Lieutenant-Commander G. T. Cooper of the *Sturdy* was subsequently to comment:

> With the exception of HGF33 which I escorted from Gibraltar, to the latitude of Finisterre last June, this was our first experience of ocean convoy work in submarine areas. I had no details of this convoy, nor did I know the nature of the escort and I had never met any of the Commanding Officers of the other ships. No plan of action in the event of attack had therefore been discussed between us.

Lieutenant-Commander Russell had never before escorted a convoy in the Western Approaches, though he had escorted numerous convoys in the Channel and on the East Coast. His ship having been out of circulation for some time past, undergoing refit, he was out of touch with events and not aware how conditions had changed since the U-boats adopted the surface attack. Later he was to admit that 'there was an entire lack of co-ordination and team work to meet this form of attack'. Perhaps the most experienced of the escorts was the *Jason*, though her experience was not such as to breed confidence. Lieutenant-Commander R. E. Terry, her captain, ruefully commented that 'in the past six weeks he had picked up no less than 720 survivors from sunken merchantmen'.

Such was the force which settled down in their stations round HX79 on the evening of the 19th October as it steered eastwards for the North Channel at 8½ knots. The convoy consisted of 49 ships. Sailing with it, and stationed in the centre was the Dutch submarine *O21*, an arrangement which was being tried out at this time as a possible defence against surface raiders.

It was a dark, overcast and drizzling night, with visibility varying between half a mile and three miles, and the moon had not yet risen, when at 9.20 p.m. the attack opened with two ships on the starboard side of the convoy being torpedoed. In the absence of any pre-arranged plan the various escorts took individual, unco-ordinated action. The *Whitehall* crossed the front of the convoy and made an asdic search of the area on the starboard flank. Reaching the rear, she made contact with the *Arabis*. For half an hour the two ships swept up and down and across the wake of the convoy. Nothing was sighted. The *Jason* then joined them and a further search was made round the two torpedoed ships which were still floating.

In spite of the presence of three trawlers, ships well suited to the work of rescue, one of the convoy, *Loch Lomond*, had been detailed to act as rescue ship. With great courage her master had at once turned to carry out this duty. Nevertheless when three men on a raft made a frenzied appeal to be picked up, Russell felt compelled to comply, though a boat-load of other survivors were instructed to row over to the *Loch Lomond* near by. Then, as starshells blossoming to the eastward indicated further happenings in the convoy, Russell sped away to investigate, leaving *Jason* to stand by the torpedoed ships.

At 11.15 p.m. there were two vivid explosions ahead. As he was making for them there was an enormous flash with flames reaching high up into the sky at a considerable distance in another quarter. Assuming it to be a tanker laden with petrol which had just been torpedoed, he turned off towards it. In fact it was a ship which had been torpedoed some days beforehand and had been burning ever since. It was an unfortunate diversion which gives some indication of how littered with burning, sinking or crippled ships were the North-Western Approaches at that time.

Finding nothing and coming to the correct conclusion that what he had seen had taken place some distance beyond the horizon, Russell resumed his course to overtake the convoy. He soon came across the trawlers *Angle* and *Lady Elsa* standing by four torpedoed ships, one of which was a burning tanker. Leaving the trawlers to do what they could, *Whitehall* hurried on, only to find yet another disabled ship with a number of lifeboats near her. Hardening his heart, Russell ignored them for the time being, though this meant leaving men in the water who were whistling and shouting for rescue. Joined now by the *Sturdy*, the *Whitehall* had barely reached the convoy when there were two more explosions. The tanker *Athel Monarch* and a freighter *Whitford Point* had been hit. The former was damaged only and eventually reached port; but the freighter went down in ten seconds.

Though the moon had risen some two hours earlier and visibility was now as much as five miles, a frantic search by *Whitehall* and *Sturdy* failed to get a sight of the enemy. There seemed nothing for Russell to do but to send *Sturdy* to rescue the struggling survivors of the *Whitford Point* while he himself took the *Whitehall* back to the help of the men he had been forced previously to abandon. Thereafter he quartered to and fro across the rear of the convoy. For a time there were no further incidents. Then at 4.20 a.m. an explosion in the far distance to port of the convoy occurred. Moving over in that direction, Russell found the *Hibiscus* in station there. This was the first time that Russell had any information as to the whereabouts of *Hibiscus*, which in fact had remained in the vicinity of the convoy throughout the night, without catching a glimpse of the enemy who were wreaking the havoc. Her captain confirmed that the explosion had been a long way off and so presumably unconnected with the convoy. In fact it was the Swedish steamer *Janus* whose master, at his crew's insistence, had broken convoy when the attacks started and had paid the inevitable penalty. He and his men were lucky to be picked up later when, during the following morning, *Hibiscus* was directed to the position by a patrolling Sunderland. Russell therefore took the *Whitehall* across the convoy to try to find out which escorts were still in company. On the starboard side he found *Heliotrope* which had also remained with the convoy throughout. Though she had circled the convoy continuously, she, too, had had no sight of an enemy. In deep despair, Russell returned to cover the rear of the convoy and to await the dawn.

There was to be yet one more calamity. Shortly before 5 a.m. the *Jason* picked up a signal from the *Loch Lomond*, left on her own after rescuing survivors, that she was being chased by a submarine. Terry at once went to her aid; but he had not yet located her when, at 7.25, a white rocket soaring up into the air told him he was too late to save her. *Loch Lomond* had been torpedoed five minutes before. Though she was still afloat when *Jason* came up with her, she was beyond hope of salvage and her crew were in their boats from which *Jason* embarked them.

It was the final loss suffered by HX79. That there would have been more on the following night, but for the fact that the U-boats had expended their torpedoes, seems certain. But it was bad enough. Twelve ships had been sunk and two more damaged, 24·5 per cent of the convoy. In SC7 the percentage had been 58·8. These two catastrophic encounters perhaps mark the very nadir of British fortunes in the Battle of the Atlantic. They were made harder to bear by the inability of the powerful escort of HX79 either to protect the convoy or exact a penalty from the U-boats. On the German side they represented the first occasion when pack tactics were employed. Their success greatly encouraged Admiral Dönitz, who had long wished to put them into use but had until then been frustrated by a shortage of operational boats. From then onwards they would be the standard tactics, to be used whenever the opportunity presented itself.

On the British side it was not all loss, however. The very completeness of the defeat of the escorts led to a strict examination of the causes and to an all-out effort to improve matters. The results will be seen in the next chapter.

4

The Opposing Forces Gather

THE CONVOY BATTLES of October 1940 could be fairly classed as catastrophic. The new German tactics of surface attack in packs by night posed a problem to which there seemed to be no answer readily available. The losses of SC7 could be explained by the swamping of the weak escort. HX79, on the other hand, had, on paper, a very strong one; yet its losses were nearly as great and, but for the expenditure of the U-boat's torpedoes, might have been worse. Furthermore, the submarines had been able to roam at will amongst the escorts and even inside the columns of the convoy, only one being detected and forced to dive. The concentrated loss from these two convoys within a period of three days brought home the seriousness of the situation in a way that more dispersed, yet equally severe losses might not have done. Something was evidently wrong with the methods—or the means—of protecting convoys. The school of thought which had never been convinced by the arguments for a convoy system began to make itself heard again.

Indeed, they had never been entirely silenced. Their views had prevailed sufficiently to lead to a number of the desperately needed destroyer escorts being wastefully employed on futile 'offensive' search and patrol, instead of as close escorts to convoys where they could be sure of encountering the enemy. This school, in defiance of the lessons of the past—chiefly, one must think, because they had never been studied—now advocated the sailing of our convoys along patrolled shipping lanes. They backed their arguments with the insidious siren song which promised an economy thereby in the use of escorts and aircraft. Fortunately, although this recommendation was approved by the Defence Committee when it sat under the Prime Minister's chairmanship to consider the convoy situation soon after the attacks on SC7 and HX79, the ever-increasing westerly spread of the area of the U-boat operations made its implementation impossible.

On the other hand it was at this time that a body known as the Import Executive persuaded the Cabinet, in spite of Admiralty protests, to reduce the upper speed limit for ships in convoy to 12·9 and later to 12 knots. As the Admiralty had predicted, the losses amongst independents soared; but it was not until June 1941 that the speed limit was restored to 14·9 knots.

As some counterpoise to this ill-considered action, the Defence Committee took the important decision that the time had come to release to trade protection duties many of the destroyers which up to then had been held on the east and south coasts against any invasion attempts by the enemy. This had the important result of leavening the slow, ill-trained sloops and corvettes which had hitherto formed the majority of the escorts with speedy vessels manned by experienced crews. Not only were these ships better equipped and trained to hunt any U-boats detected, but their high speed enabled them to cover greater areas of water round the convoy and so make the penetration of the screen by U-boats more hazardous. Furthermore they could rejoin the convoy quickly after being thrown out to aid a damaged ship or exhort a laggard, whereas, as has been seen, a corvette or sloop which once dropped behind was out of the picture for many hours. Before November was out the strengthening of the convoy escorts in this way had paid an encouraging dividend in the destruction of *U32* by the destroyers *Harvester* and *Highlander*, of *U31* by the *Antelope* and of *U104* by the corvette *Rhododendron*.

There were, however, many other duties for which destroyers were required elsewhere. Few could be spared for convoy duty. It was for this reason that Winston Churchill had been striving to persuade the Americans to release to us, in barter for base facilities in British possessions in the west, 50 over-age destroyers which were lying idle in reserve. In September 1940 he had succeeded and an agreement was signed. Though these ships were antique in armament and machinery and had to be fitted with asdics before they could be of use, they were to prove a valuable stop-gap at the height of the Battle of the Atlantic when every warship that could float and steam was beyond price.

Nevertheless it was obvious that there were many other requirements if the pack-attacks were to be defeated. Some were purely material. Radar, which had first been invented before the war, had been developed in Britain primarily as an air warning device against bombing attacks. The next variation of it had been an airborne set for reconnaissance aircraft. At the end of 1940, however, the set fitted in aircraft of Coastal Command was of very low performance and useless for anti-submarine work. The development of an improved set for aircraft and of one which could be installed in escort vessels was now given a high priority.

Another need which the convoy battles of October 1940 brought into prominence was that for better and quicker communications between the escorts. Wireless telegraphy, the only means available by night or in low visibility up to this time, was slow, each message having to be written down and encoded before transmission. It required a fully trained operator on each wave length manned. Such men did not exist in the necessary numbers; nor was there living space for them in the smaller escorts. Radio-telephony, on the other hand, was much quicker in operation and could be used by signalmen or officers of the watch or even directly between the escort commander and his commanding officers. It was also an essential means of communication between warships and aircraft. This, too, was accepted as vitally required equipment.

Finally the experiences of the commanding officers of the escorts had shown that team work by the escorts was essential to combat the obviously efficient team work which had been developed by the enemy. Commander Allen of the *Leith*, after his heartbreaking experience with SC7 had commented, 'With the present means available the difficulties of communications between the Senior Officer and other escorts in such circumstances cannot be too highly stressed—and as a corollary, the necessity for team work.' Lieutenant-Commander Russell had deplored 'the entire lack of co-ordination and team-work'.

It was to be some months yet before this eventual cardinal

principle of convoy escort work was accepted and acted upon by the formation of regularly constituted escort groups. There were already in the Western Approaches Command senior officers who had absorbed the doctrine and were working to implement it. Before they could do so, however, they had first to persuade the unsympathetic personnel departments of the Admiralty, frantically seeking to spread a thin layer of professional 'butter' on the large slices of amateur 'bread' coming forward to man the new ships of the rapidly expanding Navy, that officers and men who had convoy experience should be retained in escort vessels. And they had to fight the inevitable tendency for operational departments to take ships wherever they could find them for the multifarious duties of high priority elsewhere.

These improvements, when made, would enable the escorts to meet the U-boats on more equal terms when they moved in to the attack; but they did nothing to prevent the concentration by day which led to the subsequent pack-attack by night. Unless this could be done, the escorts could still be overwhelmed and reduced to purely passive attempts to plug the holes in the defences instead of taking the offensive.

A technical device was being developed to this end, which would take advantage of the Achilles heel of the wolf-packs—the need to use radio freely to effect their concentration. The key unit in a pack-attack was the U-boat which first made contact with a convoy. It was essential that this boat should signal the news to headquarters and thereafter shadow the convoy, reporting any alterations of route. Furthermore, as other boats came on the scene they had also to signal the fact. There were yet other occasions when boats were expected to report their positions or their inability, for one reason or another, to carry out the orders sent to them by the U-boat Command.

All these signals were made on High Frequency wireless. They could be picked up by direction-finding stations ashore, cross-bearings from several widely separated stations giving a rough position of the U-boat transmitting. This information was passed to the U-boat Tracking Room set up in the Admiralty where, as time went on, a remarkably accurate picture of U-boat dispositions came to be built up. Convoys could be warned that U-boats were in contact with them or they could be diverted to skirt round areas where it was known that U-boats were lying in wait. Efforts to develop a High Frequency Direction Finder which would function in a ship had been going on in the Royal Navy since the beginning of the war. Technical difficulties had foiled them up to this time, and though they were eventually to be overcome it was to be another year before escorts would be able to take immediate advantage of the radio chatter which was a feature of Admiral Dönitz's method of control of his forces.

To develop, produce and supply all these technical aids to escort vessels would take time. Until then the U-boats were in a position of clear advantage. Yet the prime antidote to the U-boat was immediately to hand, if it had only been appreciated. Already the U-boats were moving their patrol area farther westward to avoid the occasional Sunderland flying-boat which was all that Coastal Command could spare to quarter the sea area off the North-Western Approaches.

Aircraft were, indeed, coming from the factories in ever-increasing numbers, but a lack of appreciation of the crucial part they had to play in the defeat of the U-boats, on which all other operations of war ultimately depended, was still keeping Coastal Command the Cinderella of the R.A.F. Multi-engined aircraft went first to satisfy the demands of Bomber Command and the strategic bombing offensive on which such hopes were pinned—hopes which post-war research has shown to have been set far too high. As their contribution to the war at sea, aircraft of Bomber Command were sent out to bomb the U-boat yards and bases. Though it could not be known at the time, the effect of these raids on the U-boat offensive was negligible. Production was not slowed up nor was a single U-boat destroyed.

Shortage of aircraft was not the only obstacle to Coastal Command's efforts. The lessons of the First World War had been forgotten or not absorbed. The air crews had not received the specialised training to enable them to co-operate efficiently with the Navy, which had been found to be so essential then. And the basic principle being slowly re-learnt by the Navy, that it was in the vicinity of convoys that the U-boat could be most surely met and defeated, was never accepted by the Royal Air Force. What few aircraft were available were often wasted on patrolling the U-boat transit routes or searching enormous areas of ocean. Lacking a lethal weapon with which to attack, even the few contacts with U-boats brought no reward. Had they been attached to the convoys themselves they would have forced the shadowing U-boat to dive and lose contact, and would have prevented the concentration and positioning of the U-boat packs for which free movement on the surface was essential. Furthermore they would have achieved far more frequent contacts and, though they still had no satisfactory weapon, in conjunction with the escorts they could have harried, hunted and perhaps destroyed many of the enemy.

Thus none of the means whereby the U-boats were eventually to be mastered were available in the winter of 1940.

It was indeed fortunate, therefore, that the nature of the problem facing the convoy escorts was so clearly revealed at a time when the enemy was still too weak in numbers to exploit to the full the technique he had re-discovered. With less than 30 operational U-boats, large-scale pack operations were inevitably followed by periods of replenishment and rest for a large proportion of his available force. During November and December, 1940, no more than six U-boats operated simultaneously. Combined with winter weather and low visibility, this made interception of convoys and pack-attacks more difficult. One such attack, which took place on the 1st December on HX90, was sufficient to banish any complacency. *U99*, the boat of the ace-commander, Otto Kretschmer, his reputation enhanced by the sinking in November of the armed merchant cruisers *Laurentic* and *Patroclus,* was among the pack of four boats which got amongst the ships of the convoy and sank 11 of them including the armed merchant cruiser *Forfar.*

Though it was the German U-boat arm which was to inflict by far the greatest damage on Allied merchant shipping and thereby bring Britain closer to defeat than any other enemy activity, there were other forms of attack, far from negligible in the number of their victims, which were to stretch Britain's naval resources to the limit.

The first of these to reach serious proportions was the magnetic mine which, in the early months of the war, had claimed more victims than U-boats' torpedoes. The story of how they and the acoustic mines which followed them were countered is outside the scope of a book devoted to an account of the Battle of the Atlantic. It is a story of heroic endeavour to wrest the secret of their mechanisms from unexploded examples which fell into Allied hands, of ingenuity in producing the necessary counter-measures and of cold-blooded, nerve-wracking courage in their operation which deserves a book on its own.

The next form of attack, in point of time, to be exploited was that of the surface raiders. The cruises of the *Graf Spee* and *Deutschland* have been briefly recounted. Others were to follow them. Though the success they achieved was, in the sum, small, they constituted a permanent threat to the whole complicated convoy system and were to tie down naval strength, out of all proportion to their own, to provide a deterrent.

In October 1940, the pocket battleship *Admiral Scheer* had broken out into the Atlantic, passing undetected through the Denmark Strait. On the 5th November the homeward-bound convoy HX84 in mid-Atlantic saw her towering top-hamper rise over the horizon. Captain E. S. F. Fegen, commanding the solitary escort, the armed merchant cruiser *Jervis Bay*, signalled the order to the convoy to scatter and took his ship out to the unequal combat. Before his ancient guns were silenced and his ship sunk the convoy had had time to scatter so widely that out of the 37 ships of which it was composed the *Scheer* could round up and sink only five.

The German then steered south to begin a cruise lasting five months during which she roamed far and wide in the South Atlantic and Indian Ocean, capturing or sinking single, unescorted merchant-men before finally returning to Germany. Her total achievements were the sinking of the *Jervis Bay* and 16 merchantmen totalling 99,059 tons. It was a mere pin-prick compared to the destruction wrought by the U-boats; but her presence on the ocean, like that of the cruiser *Hipper*, and the battle-cruisers *Scharnhorst* and *Gneisenau* which followed, added to the already deep anxiety felt by the Admiralty and the Government for the safety of the vital Atlantic trade, and absorbed almost the whole of Britain's naval strength in giving it protection.

Mention has been made of a further threat to our shipping in the establishment on the French Atlantic coast of squadrons of long-range Focke-Wulf Kondor aircraft. Although, owing to friction between the Kriegsmarine and the Luftwaffe—which retained complete control of the employment and training of these and other naval co-operation aircraft—they contributed little at this time in their reconnaissance function, their depredations amongst 'independents' and stragglers from the convoys had steadily risen month by month. During November 1940 they accounted for 18 ships, totalling 66,438 tons.

The guns with which most merchant ships had been fitted as a defence against attack by surfaced U-boats were useless against aircraft. Arrangements were set afoot to gather in anti-aircraft guns from the defences of shore-establishments and mount them in merchant ships, and for crews to be trained to man them. These latter were recruited into the Admiralty's Defensively Equipped Merchant-ship (D.E.M.S.) organisation or the Maritime A.A. Regiment of the Royal Artillery. Though by the nature of things a very large number of men were thus tied up in jobs which rarely paid a concrete dividend, their presence in the otherwise unarmed ships of the Merchant Navy had an incalculable effect in stiffening morale, as many stories of their steady behaviour in adversity were to illustrate. By 1944 these two organisations were to absorb 38,000 men between them.

Another ominous sign of things to come during the winter months of 1940 was the appearance of U-boats on the route between Freetown, Sierra Leone, the convoy assembly port for the large and vital trade from the Orient, and the United Kingdom. Shipping on that route had till then escaped attack, but in December five ships were sunk off Portugal and four off Freetown. Thus there came another call for increased escort strength and for Coastal Command to extend their already fully stretched resources to that area.

It was plain that the coming of spring 1941 would see a resumption of an all-out assault on Atlantic shipping. In England the decks were being cleared in anticipation. In one of his most famous war-time speeches on the 9th February, 1941, Churchill forecast the struggle to come when he said:

We must therefore expect that Herr Hitler will do his utmost to prey upon our shipping and to reduce the volume of American supplies entering these islands.

Having conquered France and Norway, his clutching fingers reach out on both sides of us into the ocean.

The Prime Minister brought the full weight of his personality and drive to spur on the preparations and to give the U-boat war top priority over every other type of activity. Finally, on the 6th March, he issued the directive which gave the name Battle of the Atlantic to the whole wide-spread and unceasing fight. Meanwhile, Flower-class corvettes were coming from the builders' yards in a steady stream. A new headquarters for the Western Approaches Command was being set up at Liverpool and a new Commander-in-Chief and staff appointed whose efforts would be directed solely to the conduct of the U-boat war. To improve the direction of the air effort of Coastal Command, it was decided to vest its operational control in the Admiralty. This did not come into force until April 1941 nor did it give naval Commanders-in-Chief the direct control of aircraft working with their forces, which would have been the ideal; but it served to ensure the employment of Coastal Command aircraft primarily on naval co-operation which had not always been the case before.

Experience had revealed the misdirection of effort in the employ-ment of destroyers on futile search and patrol operations, when they would have been more profitably employed on convoy escort, and the weakening of the escorts themselves by the despatch, on orders from headquarters, of units to hunt U-boats reported perhaps 100 miles or more from the convoys. Search for a mouse reported in a ten-acre field had as much chance of success as these 'offensive' moves.

The consequences were brought home to Admiral Sir Percy Noble, the Commander-in-Chief designate, when he embarked in the ship of a senior officer of the escort of a convoy, and, as a result of such orders, found himself after a while in the sole remaining escort, all the others having been dispersed on various tasks. Thereafter, it was left to the senior officer of an escort to decide whether it was sound to send off any of his units.

At the beginning of the war, the only long-range escort vessels in the Royal Navy were 22 sloops similar to the *Scarborough, Fowey* and *Leith,* which we have seen trying ineffectively to cope with attacks on the convoy they were escorting. Around 1,000 tons displacement and with a maximum speed of 16 knots, they had been designed with an eye on their peacetime role as gunboats on foreign stations. The accommodation for officers and men was more adapted to the tropics than the winter in the North Atlantic; but it was their lack of speed compared to the 18 knots of their opponents which was their chief handicap. Only speed could compensate for lack of numbers. On the other hand, they had an advantage over any other small ship of the Royal Navy at that time in their long endurance, which made them the only escorts capable of remaining with a convoy throughout its voyage.

The only other ships at first available for ocean escort were the old destroyers of the 'S', 'V' and 'W' classes, veterans of the First World War, which had fortunately been maintained in reserve from the time they were relieved as fleet destroyers by the 'A' to 'I' classes of the inter-war years. They were fine, sturdy little ships and good sea-boats, capable of 30 knots and mostly fitted with an asdic set, though of an early type. The removal of the aftermost of their four 4-inch guns to make way for an increased depth-charge armament made them excellent anti-submarine ships. But they were few in number, only 60, and not all of them allocated to the Western Approaches. Furthermore, designed for war in the North Sea, their fuel stowage was meagre so that their endurance limited them to accompanying a convoy only a few hundred miles outward before turning back with an inward-bound convoy.

Their ancient machinery was a constant anxiety to their engineers who often worked miracles in keeping them running with only brief rests between spells of sea-going. Their plates burst rivets as their hulls whipped and shuddered in the huge Atlantic seas. As solid, green water swept destructively along their decks, much of it found its way down into the living spaces where it sloshed to and fro across the mess decks and cabin flats. There, in an atmosphere of thick, damp 'fugg', the crews passed the comfortless off-duty hours. Their clothes perpetually soaked, in an aroma compounded of bilge water, sweat and the last meal, they sat at the bare scrubbed mess tables or lay on the padded locker-lids. By night there were hammocks for some; but there were rarely slinging billets for the whole wartime complement of a warship. The remainder staked out claims on the lockers or mess tables.

On their tiny bridges only canvas dodgers and primitive wind-baffles gave protection to the look-outs, signalmen and watch officers from the wind, the stinging spray and the penetrating cold. On dark nights of storm, with perhaps 50 ships somewhere close by, hidden in the murk, attentions were inevitably concentrated on the avoidance of collision to the exclusion of other considerations. From this restricted platform and the little chart room below it, almost filled by the chart table and the drawers of chart folios under it, the escort commander was expected to navigate his own ship, to control his wide-spread command in keeping the convoy together, in passing orders from the Command to the Commodore and, when they came, in beating off the attacks of the enemy.

Until the advent of radar there was no rest for escort commanders or captains of ships while in U-boat haunted waters. Sleep was taken in snatches, broken by appeals from inexperienced officers of the watch who had lost touch with the convoy, by the receipt of important signals requiring immediate action, or by alarms from the asdic operators in contact with something that could be a submarine but was far more frequently a shoal of fish or a whale. A clear night, or, better still, moonlight brought some relief but sleep was never more than a short pace over the borderline of consciousness, the 'ping' of the asdic continuing to carry its unceasing enquiry to the restless brain. Any change in the even tempo of the quiet bridge routine brought instant wakefulness.

It was the 'V' and 'W' destroyers and their rather more modern sisters of the 'A' to 'I' classes which later joined them that made an immortal name for themselves and bore the brunt of the Battle of the Atlantic with the smaller, Flower-class corvettes. Backing the sturdy but elderly 'V's and 'W's were also the ex-American over-age destroyers taken over by the Royal Navy and the Royal Canadian Navy—the famous 'four-stackers' as they were commonly called. That most of them performed splendid service in filling a critical gap in our convoy defences will not be denied. At the same time it has to be recorded that to their new British owners they seemed vile little ships.

Their narrow, 'herring-gutted' lines gave them a vicious roll. Their turning circle, equivalent to that of a battleship, and, in some cases, their in-turning screws, made them too unhandy for the tight manœuvres of a submarine hunt. Their low, glass-windowed bridges made navigation difficult and look-out inefficient. When the windows were broken by heavy seas, as they sometimes were, they became almost uninhabitable. Their machinery was antiquated and un-reliable. Indeed some of the ships handed over to Britain had been headaches to their American owners before they put them away in reserve and heaved a sigh of relief.

Another type of ship which was to play a leading part in the Battle of the Atlantic was the sloop of the Black Swan class, modern ships, the first of which came to sea soon after the outbreak of war. With a speed of 19 knots and an armament of six 4-inch high-angle guns, their anti-aircraft capabilities had kept them at first with the East Coast convoys and they later played a vital part in the brief, ill-fated Norwegian campaign. When the Gibraltar convoys began to suffer heavy losses from air attack, some of these ships were transferred to that run. Later they were formed into escort groups of their own, the best known being the famous 2nd Escort Group which, under the leadership of Captain F. J. Walker, took a heavy toll amongst the U-boats.

Trawlers also played their part in swelling the numbers of escorts round convoys. Many had been taken over by the Admiralty and fitted with asdics and depth-charges. The duty which had been visualised for them had been primarily that of patrolling the approaches to ports; the desperate shortage of escorts had, how-ever, led to their transfer to escort work. Their low speed and small depth-charge armament gave them poor offensive capabilities and they achieved very few concrete successes against the U-boats. On the other hand they were able to take over from the other escorts the task of standing by crippled ships and of rescuing crews of sunken ones, thus leaving their better-equipped comrades free to hunt for and attack the enemy.

It was the Flower-class corvettes, however, designed originally for coastal convoy work only, which were now coming forward to form the hard-core of the escort groups. Named after the homely flowers of an English garden, there was nothing of floral grace about them. Chunky and broad-beamed, they looked what they were, solid, reliable craft of 1,010 tons and, when their forecastles had been lengthened from the original design, splendid sea-boats. They had an endurance which enabled them to cross the Atlantic with a convoy without refuelling. No one would claim that they were comfortable, however. Though their shorter length saved them from the shattering bumps which a destroyer suffered heading into a sea, they rolled as fiercely and at a faster tempo. Their bridges, lower down than a destroyer's, were constantly swept by spray. Officers' cabins were tiny cupboards, the mess decks austere and wet.

They were powered by single reciprocating engines which gave them a maximum speed of 15 knots. This was insufficient to overhaul a U-boat on the surface and so limited their offensive value. On the other hand their extreme handiness made them excellent hunters of a submerged U-boat and many successes were to be marked up to their credit. But it was the numbers in which they were produced in a short time, at a period when escorts were desperately needed, that gave them their peculiar value. Speedily constructed in dozens of small shipyards all round Britain, they came forward at a rate impossible for the construction of destroyers. Four or five were allocated to each escort group, constituting the hard core of the close escort and leaving any destroyers present free to make high speed sorties to drive off or attack shadowers, to round up stragglers and to carry out the multifarious other duties round a convoy at sea. It was the hundred or more of these splendid little craft, coming to sea during the latter half of 1940 and the early spring of 1941, which gave the best assurance that the expected enemy offensive would be held.

For on the German side, too, preparations were going ahead. The

U-boat building programme was getting into its stride. By April Dönitz would have 100 boats in commission, though the need to work up new crews to operational efficiency and to train others for the 230 further boats nearing completion would keep the number in the 'front line' down to about 30 at first. Nevertheless, judging by past results, this should be enough to strike a staggering blow at the convoys.

5

The Escorts Strike Back

THE GERMAN NAVAL STAFF were well aware that merchant ships, and the ability to keep them safe, were vital to the British Commonwealth for, as Sir Winston Churchill has said, 'Without ships we cannot live, and without ships we cannot conquer'. Grand-Admiral Raeder therefore planned to use every weapon at his disposal to destroy Britain's merchant fleet. To this end he had been pressing for the Air Reconnaissance Group—Group 40, of Focke-Wulf Kondors—to be placed under the operational control of the Flag Officer U-boats. On the 7th January, 1941, Hitler approved of this; but in the following month reversed his decision. Nevertheless, it had been a clear warning to the Luftwaffe that its independence was at stake. The Commander of Group 40 thereafter took pains to co-operate whole-heartedly with the U-boat Command, with a resultant increasing success in combined operations.

At first, however, they assumed a shape different from that which had been visualised by Admiral Dönitz. Owing to lack of training in naval co-operation and poor navigation, it was not the aircraft which located convoys and directed the U-boats on to them: it was usually the other way about. On the 9th February, for instance, it was *U37*, commanded by Korvetten-Kapitän Oerhn, which first sighted the homeward-bound Gibraltar convoy HG53, 160 miles south-west of Cape St. Vincent. Having gone in to the attack on his own and sunk two ships, Oerhn then homed six F.-W. Kondors which bombed and sank a further five. After torpedoing another ship the following day, he tried also to direct the cruiser *Admiral Hipper* to the scene. Though the cruiser failed to find the convoy, she was able to pick up a straggler from it. In the same month, farther north, Günther Prien fell in with the west-bound Atlantic convoy OB290. Ordered to await the arrival of his fellow 'ace', Otto Kretschmer, in *U99*, before attacking, his accurate reports also enabled six F.-W. Kondors to find the target. While the submarines' torpedoes accounted for three ships, bombs from the aircraft sank nine and damaged two more. On the other hand it had been a successful reconnaissance by a F.-W. Kondor which a week earlier had led a U-boat to convoy OB288. The submarine then called up others and, when the escort departed on crossing the twentieth west meridian and the convoy dispersed, the wolf-pack fell on it, sinking nine ships.

The Grand-Admiral's other arm was his surface fleet of warships and armed raiders. The latter had been keeping up desultory operations in long cruises which took them to every ocean of the world. Though they were to remain a thorn in the flesh for over two years more, and were to absorb considerable naval forces devoted to efforts to round them up, their depredations were small in comparison to those of U-boats and were carried out in areas remote from the North Atlantic. They are, therefore, omitted from this volume. The larger warships of the German fleet were, on the other hand, intended to operate on the Atlantic convoy routes. There, once they had broken out into the ocean, they posed a serious threat, forcing the Admiralty to employ valuable and irreplaceable heavy ships on convoy escort duty—where they were at once easy prey for U-boats. Boldly handled, these warship raiders could bring about a naval disaster of the first magnitude.

At the turn of the year only the pocket battleship, *Admiral Scheer*, was at large. The heavy cruiser *Hipper* had been damaged in a brush with the escort of a troop convoy on Christmas Day 1940 and was repairing in Brest. She would be ready for sea again by the end of January. So, too, would be the battle cruisers *Scharnhorst* and *Gneisenau* which, since the Norwegian Campaign, had been repairing battle damage at Kiel. Carrying out trials in the Baltic were the heavy cruiser *Prinz Eugen* and Hitler's pride, the giant battleship *Bismarck*. As each of these various units was completed, they were to break out into the Atlantic. Joined together, as a squadron, they would comprise a force which would more than match that available to the Commander-in-Chief, Home Fleet.

Such was Grand-Admiral Raeder's hope. Had he waited for all his units to be ready and sent them out in company it might have been fulfilled. But *Bismarck* and *Prinz Eugen* could not be ready until April. In the meantime the remainder were sent out piece-meal. The first to sail were the *Scharnhorst* and *Gneisenau* with the flag of Vice-Admiral Lütjens, Commander-in-Chief of the German Fleet, in the latter. On the 4th February they passed through the Denmark Strait, west of Iceland, and proceeded to a prearranged rendezvous south of Greenland where oilers waited to refuel them. By the 6th February, Lütjens was ready to begin operations and was making for the route of the Halifax convoys. Two days later dawn revealed the masts of HX106 on the horizon. The two battle cruisers moved confidently in to the attack.

Then, amongst the array of pole-masts of merchantmen, was suddenly sighted the fighting top of a battleship. Though the Home Fleet had been unable to prevent the break-out of *Scharnhorst* and *Gneisenau*, their presence in the Atlantic was known. Only the slow and elderly battleship *Ramillies* could be spared to escort HX106. But it was enough. It was no part of Lütjens' plan to risk damage to either of his ships a thousand miles from base. They were more than a match for *Ramillies*, but a lucky hit from one of her 15-inch shells could bring their cruise to an untimely end. Lütjens sheered away and returned to his refuelling position while the alarm died down. Not until the 17th February did he return to the convoy route.

For four days he sighted nothing. Then at dawn on the 22nd his luck changed. Some 650 miles west of Newfoundland he found himself in sight of a number of merchantmen, widely dispersed and sailing unescorted. They were from an outward-bound convoy which, as was the unavoidable custom at that time owing to shortage of escorts, had been dispersed on reaching the limit of the U-boat area. Five of them, totalling 25,784 tons, were sunk. Several ships had been able to get distress messages on the air and in spite of jamming by the Germans, one was picked up by a shore station. Realising that shipping would now be diverted from that area, Lütjens steered south and having refuelled in mid-Atlantic, appeared off the African coast on the 8th March. There, 350 miles north of the Cape Verde Islands, he once again encountered a convoy escorted by a battleship, this time the *Malaya*. As before he refused to get involved. Instead he signalled the position of the convoy for the benefit of U-boats working in the area with the result that two of them made contact and sank five ships.

Having advertised his presence in that area, Lütjens once more crossed the Atlantic. On the 15th March the two battle-cruisers arrived in the most productive area they were to enjoy, some 200 miles to the south-east of Cape Race, an area through which ships dispersed from outward-bound Atlantic convoys were bound to pass unless widely diverted. In two days 16 of them, totalling 82,000 tons, were destroyed.

It was the final success of the cruise. At the end of it Lütjens set course for Brest where he arrived on the 22nd March to receive congratulatory messages from Raeder. The cruise had certainly been a most successful one. Apart from the not inconsiderable total of 115,622 tons of shipping destroyed, the presence of the two battle-cruisers in the Atlantic had for a time completely disrupted the whole complex cycle of convoys with a consequent serious drop in vital imports to Britain.

It was never to be repeated, however. From the moment the *Scharnhorst* and *Gneisenau* secured in the harbour of Brest they came under the constant surveillance and repeated attacks of the Royal Air Force. The former ensured that they would be intercepted if they sailed again. The latter consisted primarily of attacks by Bomber Command which, though they failed to damage either of the battle-cruisers, had the effect of slowing down the refit of the *Scharnhorst* and delaying her readiness for sea. It was not until a torpedo aircraft of Coastal Command, piloted by Flying Officer K. Campbell, penetrated to the harbour and, at the cost of his life and those of his crew, got a torpedo home in *Gneisenau*, that either ship was directly damaged. In addition an intensive minelaying campaign by aircraft of Coastal and Bomber Command and by the minelayer *Abdiel* blocked the exit from Brest for long periods. Thus Grand-Admiral Raeder's dream of a simultaneous foray by the battle-cruisers and the *Bismarck* and *Prinz Eugen* was shattered.

In the meantime the *Hipper* had also been at large during February. Her low endurance, however, had greatly restricted her movements.

Sailing on the 1st February, it was not until the 9th that she left her refuelling rendezvous to make for the Sierra Leone convoy route. There, as has been related, she was homed on to a convoy homeward-bound from Gibraltar by a U-boat which, in conjunction with Focke-Wulf Kondors, had been attacking it. This attempt at co-operation failed, and *Hipper* found only a single straggler from the convoy, which she sank on the 11th February. But ranging farther afield she had the fortune to fall in with a group of 19 ships, homeward bound from Freetown, whose escort had not yet joined them. Though the ships promptly scattered, seven of them were caught and sunk. After this achievement *Hipper* returned to Brest and a month later sailed for home for a badly needed refit.

Thus the comparative lull in U-boat operations which the opening months of 1941 had seen—a lull caused largely by the severe winter weather which made very difficult the location and shadowing of convoys and the subsequent concentration of U-boats necessary for employment of pack-tactics—was offset by the successful sorties of Raeder's surface warships, and the increasing effectiveness of the aircraft of Group 40. The success of Admiral Lütjens' foray with the battle-cruisers strengthened Grand-Admiral Raeder's ambition to proceed with a similar operation with *Bismarck* and *Prinz Eugen*. Lütjens was called home to hoist his flag in the battleship. Though *Scharnhorst* and *Gneisenau* could not be got ready to join him, as originally planned, he was ordered to sail as soon as the other two ships were battle-worthy.

This came about on the 18th May, 1941, on which date Lütjens left Gdynia on the great adventure to which Raeder pinned such high hopes. Its story has been fully told elsewhere and space does not permit its repetition in any detail in this volume. It is sufficient to record that having sunk the British battle-cruiser *Hood* and damaged the battleship *Prince of Wales* in a brief, brilliant action near the Denmark Strait, the *Bismarck* was hunted down, crippled by torpedo aircraft from *Ark Royal* and thereafter sunk by an over-whelming concentration of ships of the Home Fleet.

Prinz Eugen, after lurking in mid-Atlantic for a few days, succeeded in reaching Brest; but she had accomplished nothing. Thus the *Bismarck* operation had entirely failed to achieve its object. Though the loss of the *Hood* was a severe blow to the pride and strength of the Royal Navy, Britain's merchant shipping, as Raeder well understood, was her Achilles heel. This had not been touched. Indeed the fate of the *Bismarck* was a clear demonstration that the heyday of the battleship was nearly done. The advance in naval aviation and the increase in Britain's carrier strength was to make any repetition of such adventures impossible.

It was still—and it would remain—the U-boat which was the most effective weapon in the armoury of the German Navy. Though January 1941 showed a drop in its destructive achievements to a total of 21 ships of 162,782 tons, of which only three were actually in convoy, and in February the score rose only to 39 ships (nine of them in convoy)—a little more than half that of the previous October —an ominous feature was the absence of any U-boat sinkings during those two months. The number which would be ready for the expected spring offensive was thus increasing rapidly.

Some of the steps being taken to counter it have been told. Few of them would be ready by March. Destroyers of the Western Approaches Command were, indeed, beginning to sprout weird metal structures at their mastheads resembling large wire mattresses. These first radar aerials were not rotatable. From them went out a steady radar beam. The return signal from a target in the vicinity could be expected, if all went well, to appear as a peak in the wavering, dancing band of grass-like green light running across the screen. The range of the target could be estimated to a fair degree of accuracy. Its direction could only be guessed from a consideration of the height of the 'peak', a guess which depended for accuracy on the experience of the operators and the correct adjustment of an instrument only partially understood by them. Such was the state of development of radar for small ships of the Royal Navy 18 months after the outbreak of war; whereas ships of the German Navy had been equipped with an efficient gunnery ranging set from the beginning. The principal advantage conferred by this radar set was an ability to keep rough station in the convoy screen without being able to see any of the ships of the convoy. Previously the attention of the officer of the watch and of his look-outs on a dark night had been largely absorbed in keeping station on a dimly discernible black shape, which was the nearest ship of the convoy, and in avoiding collisions. Now at least for some of the time it would be possible to concentrate on searching for U-boats on the surface.

The chance of detecting a surfaced U-boat with this first radar set was a slim one. It was still necessary to see it and then to try to ram it. This might be successful, in which case the hunt was over at once—at a cost of a crumpled bow and the ship out of action for several weeks. More likely it would force the submarine to dive, when the asdic came into its own and enabled depth-charges to be sent down towards the target. The first essential, however, was a sight of the U-boat. Star shells had proved ineffective. Not only did they give insufficient illumination but the flash of the gun firing them completely blinded the officers and look-outs on the bridge for a space and greatly reduced the efficiency of their night-vision for some time after. While awaiting the development of an efficient radar set, it was therefore in the direction of a better illuminant that research was directed. Rockets seemed to give the required answer. A type which burst to leave a brilliant white light hanging in the sky, given the name 'Snowflake', was to be issued in May to merchant ships. At a given signal every ship would fire one of these, thus, it was hoped, turning night into day.

A better radar set for aircraft of Coastal Command was also now beginning to be fitted, enabling them to contribute by night as well as by day to convoy defence.

At the same time, radio-telephony was becoming available for communication between escorts and between escorts and aircraft. It was of limited reliability and, being on a wave in the high-frequency band and, so, unlimited in range, had to be used with caution as its signals could be picked up by monitoring stations in enemy territory. Not until after the entry of the United States into the war, when the excellent VHF radio-telephone called TBS (Talk Between Ships) became a standard fitting in all escorts, was there the free, reliable and rapid inter-communication so essential to co-ordinated team-work.

Finally, from the ever-increasing number of escorts in the Western Approaches Command organised groups were being formed. Usually these consisted of two destroyers, one of which would be commanded by the group leader, a Commander, R.N., and perhaps six Flower-class corvettes. On the convoy route to Gibraltar and Freetown, where the danger of air attack was greatest, anti-aircraft sloops of the Stork class were included and one of these was usually the ship of the group commander. Allowing for refits and repairs from weather or action damage, it was hoped to have six ships from each group always in sea-going condition.

Though there was little opportunity, as yet, for these groups to exercise and practise together—the tempo of the convoy schedule gave insufficient breathing-space between operations—the very fact that the commanding officers got to know one another, that the group commander knew their respective abilities (or, indeed, lack of them) and was able to convey to them in general terms what he expected of them under varying circumstances, built up the essential team spirit. In the blackness of stormy nights, with the convoy becoming dispersed as each master handled his ship differently in the grip of heavy seas, the group commander could be satisfied that the little corvettes hanging round the flanks would keep in touch and do everything possible to keep the convoy together. When the thud of torpedo explosions and the soaring of distress rockets announced the opening of an attack, each ship of the group would know what was expected of them, brief messages over the radio telephone would keep all members of the team informed as to the situation.

The results of these several improvements were soon to be seen. Convoy battles had been few in January and February, 1941, partly owing to the convoys being diverted far to the north, almost to Iceland, so as to by-pass the U-boat patrol lines. This soon became apparent to the U-boat Command. In the first days of March the submarine concentration was moved to the area south of Iceland.

Dönitz's most experienced and skilful commanders were soon in action. Once again it was the luck of Günther Prien in U_{47} to be the first to sight the outward-bound OB293. His luck had not much further to run, however—or perhaps it was not potent enough to balance a no-longer valid contempt for the forces against him. His signals brought his fellow 'ace' Otto Kretschmer on to the scene in *U99*, together with Matz in *U70*, Eckermann in *UA* and others. After dark they closed confidently in for the kill.

Torpedoes thudded as they found their mark and rockets told their tragic tale. So far the story was the familiar one. The Sunderland flying boat on patrol in the area had occasionally forced the U-boats to dive as they had gathered round during the previous day; but, lacking any lethal weapon with which to attack, it had been only a temporary inconvenience. Without radar the escorts had been unable to prevent the wolves from slinking past them in the darkness. But thereafter the story changed. There was a new sense of purpose and an evident increase of skill amongst the escorts. *UA* was forced to dive in a hurry, was detected by an escort's asdic and so damaged by depth charges that Eckermann was forced to disengage and set course for his base. Then *U70* was caught by the corvettes *Camellia* and *Arbutus*. Heavy damage to his boat forced Matz to surface and surrender with most of his crew before *U70* went down for the last time. *U99* was forced to dive and withdraw with half of her torpedoes unexpended, an unusual experience for Otto Kretschmer. The convoy steamed on after suffering the comparatively light loss of two ships sunk and two damaged.

Prien, as was his duty, continued to shadow the convoy. Overbold, he ventured too close. The destroyer *Wolverine*, commanded by Commander J. M. Rowland, came suddenly on him as a sheltering rain squall cleared. *U47* crash-dived but depth-charges damaged her propeller shafts. Surfacing after dark in the hope of escaping the destroyer, which had clung persistently to an intermittent asdic contact, the submarine's propellers emitted a rattle clearly to be heard on *Wolverine*'s asdic, leading her accurately to the target. Further depth-charge attacks shattered *U47*'s hull. A vivid flash and an explosion from the depths told of her end, confirmed as wooden debris floated to the surface. As Dönitz's obituary notice was later to record, 'The hero of Scapa Flow has made his last patrol. We of the U-boat service proudly mourn and salute him and his men. . . .'

That night the survivors of the wolf-pack heard the Command ordering all U-boats in the area to report their positions. One by

one they replied, all except *U70* and *U47*. They feared for the fate
of their comrades. They were not left long to contemplate it, however. On the evening of the 12th March there came once again the
signal reporting a homeward-bound convoy south of Iceland, a rich
bait comprising nearly 50 fine, deeply laden freighters and tankers,
which must surely draw every U-boat in the area towards it. The
boat from which the signal came was *U110*, commanded by
Korvetten-Kapitän Lemp, who had opened the U-boat war on the
3rd September, 1939, by sinking the liner *Athenia*.

Among the boats which acted on Lemp's report were *U99* and
U100, the latter commanded by Joachim Schepke, Kretschmer's
friendly rival for first place in the list of tonnage sunk. The escort
with the convoy was unusually powerful in the quality of the ships
of which it was composed—five destroyers and two corvettes. With
five fast ships quartering to and fro, the problem of getting through
the screen was made more difficult for the U-boats.

The first to go into the attack on the night of the 15th March
could deliver only a long-range attack from outside the screen before
withdrawing, having sunk one ship, the only success during that
night. Nothing further occurred during the day which followed to
indicate to the escort commander that a wolf-pack was gathering
until, shortly before dusk, a shadowing submarine was sighted on
the horizon. This was *U100*. Three destroyers raced away to hunt
it, to attack it if contact could be gained on their asdics and to keep
it down while in the gathering darkness the convoy turned away to
a fresh course, which it was hoped might throw the U-boats off the
trail. For two hours the destroyers searched without result, before
leaving to rejoin the convoy.

Meanwhile the reduced strength of the escort had enabled
Kretschmer to move in undetected and employ his usual deadly
technique from amongst the columns of merchant ships. When
explosions, rockets and the ghastly glare from burning tankers
resulted, the escorts searched in vain, on the outskirts, for a sight of
their enemy. For all the speed of the destroyers, now coming up to
full strength as the hunters of *U100* rejoined, for all the experience
of the captains of the escorts, several of them veterans of the convoy
war, it seemed that the U-boat's immunity was unshakeable. Five

ships were torpedoed. No news of any U-boat sighting came to the distracted escort commander.

Yet the basic virtue of the convoy system was about to be demonstrated: that it is in the immediate vicinity of the convoy, the lure to which every U-boat must come if it is to achieve its purpose, that the submarines are in greatest peril. Resisting the temptation to cast wildly about, firing starshells, as had been the tactics in the past, the escorts kept doggedly to their stations and prayed for a gleam of fortune.

It came with the arrival of *U100*, pounding after the convoy at high speed, the brash, over-confident Schepke determined to have his share in yet another massacre such as that of SC7. His bow-wave betrayed him to look-outs on the bridge of the destroyer *Walker*, ship of the escort commander. A crash-dive saved him from being rammed. But a long hunt by *Walker* and the destroyer *Vanoc* finally forced *U100* to the surface to be rammed and sunk by *Vanoc*. Another 'ace', a hero of the U-boat arm, had followed Prien. The sea-wolves' ill-luck had not yet exhausted itself—ill-luck combined in some degree with a lack of caution bred by repeated encounters with an ill-trained and inexperienced enemy.

U99's torpedoes expended, Kretschmer had safely disengaged from the convoy and was circling round on the surface astern of it to set course for his base. Kretschmer himself, well satisfied with his night's work, had gone below, leaving the bridge in the charge of a junior officer. Suddenly there were sighted ahead the black silhouettes of two destroyers, one of them evidently stopped. They were, in fact, the *Vanoc*, stopped and picking up a handful of survivors from *U100*, and *Walker*, circling her to give her protection. With the usual advantage of the first sighting, *U99* could have swung away and escaped unseen. Instead the officer of the watch ordered an immediate crash dive. As the submarine submerged, the asdic beam from the *Walker* picked her up. An accurately delivered pattern of depth-charges wrecked her machinery and inflicted other vital damage. No alternative was left to Kretschmer but to surface while he could and surrender. He and all but two of his crew were soon prisoners aboard the *Walker*, and *U99* had followed her interminable succession of victims to the bottom.

The loss of these four boats within a week, coming after a long period of complete immunity, and of the three most successful commanders, gave Admiral Dönitz food for serious thought. Had some new anti-submarine device been developed, he wondered. Until the other boats of the pack returned and their commanders could be interrogated, he could not tell. It seemed prudent however to shift his boats from the area south of Iceland where all the losses had occurred. By shifting them in a south-westerly direction, he gave them a no longer passage to their operational area, while at the same time they would be working beyond the westerly limit to which escorts based in Britain could go without refuelling.

The move was at once successful. Encountering SC26 to the south-east of Greenland before its Western Approaches escort had met it, the U-boats sank 10 ships out of the total of 22 in convoy. To counter this move, the Admiralty based escort groups in Iceland which took over the escort of convoys from the home-based escorts from south of Iceland to 35 degrees west, and brought homeward-bound convoys from 35 degrees west to a rendezvous with home-based escorts for the last part of their journey.

Thus the battle spread ever westwards. It was soon apparent that the time was coming when continuous escort would have to be provided clear across the Atlantic. How to do this was a knotty problem. None of the destroyers used on escort duty had sufficient endurance to remain with a convoy even as far as Newfoundland. Refuelling at sea was a seaman-like art which had been regrettably neglected by the Royal Navy in the years of peace. Equipment suitable for North Atlantic weather was being devised, but it was not until June 1942 that it came regularly to be used, after which it became an essential feature of every escort problem. Nor were there sufficient escorts to permit groups to be based in Canada or Newfoundland to take care of the western portion of the trans-Atlantic journey.

The Royal Canadian Navy had been only a token force comprising seven destroyers and five minesweepers at the beginning of the war. The destroyers had gone at once to swell the ranks of the Royal Navy during the early months of the war, while great efforts were made to expand the Canadian Navy so that it might take its part as soon as possible in the Atlantic battle. Corvettes built in Canadian shipyards were soon being commissioned. When the 50 American over-age destroyers were released to Britain, seven of them were taken over and manned by Canadians. By the end of May 1941, enough Canadian escorts were in commission, based for the most part at St. John's, Newfoundland, and comprising the Newfoundland Escort Force, for a weak escort to be provided between the Canadian coast and longitude 35 degrees west, where a Mid-Ocean Meeting Point was allocated. There a group based in Iceland would take over the escort while the Canadian group would transfer to a west-bound convoy for the last part of its journey. At an Eastern Ocean Meeting Point, about 18 degrees west, a home-based group would relieve the Iceland group. The first convoy to sail eastwards so escorted was HX129 on the 27th May. In July the reverse process was inaugurated when west-bound trans-Atlantic convoys were given escort throughout their journey. A new nomenclature for them came into being at the same time, the OB convoys becoming ONF (fast) and ONS (slow). The system was highly complicated and liable to disruption owing to delays to convoys on account of bad weather or wide diversions round danger areas. It was the best, however, which could at this time be devised.

A further measure of protection for convoys was at this time provided by the establishment in Iceland of a squadron of twin-engined Hudson aircraft of Coastal Command and a squadron of Sunderland flying-boats. This provided a welcome westward extension of air cover which the U-boats found distinctly irksome. Nevertheless the number of aircraft available to Coastal Command was still far below requirements. In an effort to use those they had more effectively it was decided to take advantage of the increasingly reliable signal intelligence, by concentrating them in the vicinity of convoys which were thought to be threatened, instead of trying to give every convoy some measure of air escort. This might have been more successful had the tendency not persisted to employ much of the available air strength on offensive sweeps and searches, never very effective and less so at this stage of the war than later owing to the lack of any lethal weapon with which to attack any U-boat sighted.

Thus in May, when the U-boats returned to the area south of Iceland, no less than seven U-boats were able to gather round convoy OB318—an impossibility if there had been an air escort to keep them down during daylight hours. The loss of nine ships sunk and two others damaged was barely made up for by the capture of Lemp's *U110*, which surrendered after being depth-charged to the surface by the destroyers *Bulldog* and *Broadway*, and the corvette *Aubretia*. Though *U110* sank while in tow before she could be got to port, documents of such value and importance were recovered from her as to make the event one of the most significant of the Atlantic campaign.

Nevertheless the unusual strength of the escort encountered so far to the west as a consequence of the reinforcement from the Iceland base, and the air patrols in the area, led the U-boat command to shift its North Atlantic concentration again. The steadily increasing size and efficiency of the escort forces, sea and air, and the growing effectiveness of the U-boat tracking organisation in the Admiralty, which enabled the convoys to be diverted round danger areas, were indeed making the North Atlantic a less profitable area of operations. The first 'Happy Time' for the U-boat commanders was over. Though spectacular successes were still achieved from time to time against convoys intercepted far to the west, before an adequate escort had joined them, the submarines spent long, fruitless periods contemplating an empty ocean, while convoys passed clear of them to arrive at their destinations unscathed.

In May 1941, following the attack on OB318, the U-boats waited for a week, some 350 miles to the south-east of Cape Farewell, and sighted nothing. Moved another 240 miles south-west, towards Newfoundland, it was a further four days before convoy HX126 was intercepted, nine ships being lost from it. There followed several weeks of inactivity in the area off Newfoundland. It was not until the 20th June that a wide sweep north-eastwards to the area between Iceland and Greenland enabled *U203* to intercept HX133. The widely spread U-boat patrol line of 10 boats was called in and they were able to sink six ships and damage two more before escort reinforcements from Iceland arrived, to sink two of them and drive off the remainder. More frequent convoy interceptions would have been possible had the U-boats been free to press farther west and south to the area south of Halifax. But this would have taken them into the 'Security Zone' declared by the United States Government. Hitler's anxiety to keep the Americans neutral barred this area to the U-boats.

On the whole, therefore, the westward shift had not given the success which had been expected. The U-boat Command sought for a reason. Though its strength had been increasing since February 1941, slowly at first and sharply from May onwards, sinkings had not increased correspondingly. In July, indeed, they actually decreased considerably, though by then Dönitz had at his disposal three or four times as many boats as in January 1941.

This was to a great extent owing to the introduction in July of end-to-end anti-submarine escort of Atlantic convoys which has been mentioned above. As a result the ocean was at once swept bare of the many ships sailing independently after dispersal from their convoys, which had previously provided so rich and easy a harvest. At the same time improvement in convoy defence measures, and the growing skill and experience of the escort commanders, was not appreciated. It was not realised how very scanty and ill-found had been the escorts which the 'aces' had so contemptuously brushed aside during the 'Happy Time'. Dönitz therefore sought for a more technical reason for the decreased successes. Against the possibility of a leakage of information, security with regard to communications in the U-boat Command was tightened up.

The possibility that signals were being monitored and deciphered was considered but was scouted in the belief that German cyphers were unbreakable. On the other hand, it was known that the British were making considerable use of Direction-Finding Stations to pin-point any ship transmitting on radio. For a long time it was thought that the results were too inaccurate to matter. Wishful thinking no doubt played a part in this belief; for any restriction of the use of radio struck at the roots of the wolf-pack tactics. Now, however, half-hearted efforts to reduce the amount of signalling were made in a Standing Order issued in June 1941. Radio was to be used only for messages of tactical importance or on request from the Command, or if the enemy was already aware of the U-boats' positions. This order, however, had little effect on the volume of signals being made, as most messages from a U-boat at sea could be classified as of 'tactical importance'. Furthermore the Command itself constantly called for reports of positions necessary for the exercise of centralised control, which was the basis of Dönitz's system. A further order establishing a number of new wave-lengths and ordering the U-boats to vary them in their messages caused only temporary inconvenience in the shore-based Direction-Finding Stations, though it was to be of some consequence when H/F D/F sets began to be installed in escorts.

Technical explanations of his U-boats' decreasing success did not altogether convince Dönitz. It began to be appreciated that the easy times had gone. Pushing westwards in search of independently sailing merchant ships or lightly escorted convoys had paid a poor dividend. The dispatch of boats to the Freetown area in search of similar easy prey was temporarily very successful. Eight submarines intercepted and sank no less than 81 unescorted ships before a tightening up of convoy measures achieved the usual sharp reduction of sinkings. Furthermore, though sinkings per boat were greater there than in the north, the long passage out and home made it less profitable.

Until July 1941 this was to some extent offset by the ability of the German submarines to obtain fuel and supplies at Las Palmas in the Canary Islands. Two supply ships, *Charlotte Schliemann* and *Corrientes*, had lain there since September 1939. With the connivance of the Spanish authorities, U-boats had regularly put in at night, re-fuelled and sailed again before daylight. Strong protests by the British Government then induced the Spaniards to withdraw these facilities. Other supply ships, stationed in the Central Atlantic in support of surface raiders, had also been occasionally used to replenish U-boats. But in May 1941 the first to be used exclusively for them, the *Egerland*, was dispatched to the area. Carrying large numbers of torpedoes as well as fuel, she had not been long on station when she was intercepted by the cruiser *London* and sunk. In June 1941 no less than five other supply ships were sent out. Each was caught and destroyed. The Germans then abandoned, for the time being, the attempt to supply their submarines by this method.

Thus the effort to redress the balance by going westwards and southwards proving unsuccessful, it seemed that only by fighting their way through the convoy defence—a thing which had usually been avoided up to now when possible—could the attack on Allied merchant shipping be carried on by submarines. In July, therefore, all boats were concentrated once again in the Western and South-Western Approaches to the British Isles where it was expected that the combination of the Focke-Wulf Kondor aircraft and U-boats might enable the successes of 1940 to be renewed.

6

The Battle Spreads Westwards

THE SUMMER OF 1941 marked the end of the first phase of U-boat ascendancy on the Atlantic convoy routes. The increasing strength of the Allied escort forces which permitted continuous escort to be given to the Atlantic convoys throughout their voyages, the greater efficiency of many of the escorts as a result of experience and training, the steady spread of the air cover which Coastal Command could provide, all combined to send the U-boat packs probing in first one direction and then another to find easier targets. When they failed to find them, it was decided that there was nothing for it but to accept action with the escorts in order to get at the merchant ships in their charge. In this case there seemed little point in sending the U-boats on their long journey to the other side of the Atlantic when numerous rich targets, the convoys on the Gibraltar and Free-town routes, were to be found only a few hundred miles out at sea.

A further reason for this eastwards move had arisen through German anxiety not to become involved in incidents with ships of the United States Navy. Since the extension to 26 degrees west, in March 1941, of the 'Security Zone' patrolled by ships of the U.S. Atlantic Fleet, the risk had existed of darkened warships attacked proving to be American. In June, therefore, orders were issued restricting U-boat attacks on warships to clearly identifiable enemy cruisers, battleships and aircraft-carriers. This was a severe embarrassment to U-boat commanders who could no longer attack destroyers or corvettes even in the course of convoy battles. An appeal by Raeder to the Führer for a cancellation of this order was unsuccessful; but in August it was amended to allow attacks on destroyers and smaller warships provided they were within the original German blockade area declared in August 1940.

The coming into force of the Lend-Lease Bill in March 1941, with its consequent transfer to the Royal Navy of 10 U.S. coast-guard cutters, the arrangement whereby British warships were repaired and refitted in American yards, the relief of the British garrison in Iceland by American troops in July, followed by the announcement that U.S. naval forces would escort shipping of any nationality to and from Iceland, all made it clear that the United States were moving steadily towards active participation on the Allied side. In spite of this the restrictive order to U-boats remained in force until the entry of America into the war and for the time being the western half of the Atlantic was abandoned by the U-boats.

The shift eastwards was not a success. Not only was the operational area within range of aircraft of Coastal Command, but the U-boat commanders found that the surface escorts were too numerous and too effective. They discovered that there was now often an inner and an outer screen to penetrate before they could get within torpedo range of the merchant ships. Furthermore the position had been reversed, in that the U-boats were manned by the young and inexperienced crews who had taken the place of the early professionals who had all been killed, taken prisoner or withdrawn from operational duty; whereas it was the escort crews who were now becoming the skilled veterans.

Thus something of a stalemate developed with few successful attacks being made on the convoys, but few U-boats being sunk. While this lull held the forces on both sides were growing in strength. By the end of August the total number of U-boats in commission was 198, of which 80 were operational, figures which were steadily rising. On the Allied side, besides a steady growth in the number of escorts, there had occurred a number of developments which were to have a profound effect on the course of the campaign. The losses from bombing by the F.-W. 200 aircraft, against which the gunfire of the escorts was ineffective, had led to the fitting out of fighter catapult ships. Four of these naval auxiliaries—merchant ships fitted with a catapult from which a fighter aircraft could be launched—were commissioned by the Royal Navy in April 1941.

After completing his mission the pilot had to return to a shore base if there was one within range; otherwise he had either to 'ditch' his aircraft alongside a ship or bale out and hope to be picked up. Though it was not until August 1941 that concrete success came their way, when the Hurricane from one of them, the *Maplin*, shot down a F.-W. 200 some 400 miles out in the Atlantic, the idea had been followed up by the fitting of catapults to a number of freighters which came to be known as Catapult Aircraft Merchant-men or CAM-ships, which were to render valuable service until the advent of escort aircraft-carriers made them redundant.

The first of these auxiliary carriers also joined the escort forces at this time. This was *Audacity*, captured from the Germans as the liner *Hanover*, and fitted with a flight-deck and a hangar. Even before her brief career—in which we shall meet her shortly—had demonstrated the inestimable value of such ships, five more had been sent to British yards for conversion and six ordered from the United States under Lend-Lease arrangements. Unfortunately, for the course of the Battle of the Atlantic, it was quickly appreciated that they could fill a vital gap in the air cover for other operations as well; so that, except for *Audacity*'s inclusion in the escort of Gibraltar convoys, where she was primarily used to provide fighter defence, it was not until the winter of 1942 that a carrier sailed with a convoy on the Arctic run to Russia. The trans-Atlantic convoys were to be left without this decisive addition to their escorts until the spring of 1943.

Meanwhile the shore-based aircraft of Coastal Command had at last been equipped with the depth-charge. Results were at first disappointing. Investigation showed that the tactics being used with them were faulty. Dropped singly, the degree of accuracy required was too high. By releasing them several at a time in quick succession —or in a 'stick' as the airmen's jargon had it—there was a good chance of straddling the target and greatly increasing the destructive effect. Furthermore, the charges were set to burst too deep. The crucial moment for a submarine detected by an aircraft was when it was just taking the plunge to safety in the depths. It was still visible but neither on the surface, where the effect of a depth-charge was greatly lessened, nor deep, where the three-dimensional problem made placing a depth-charge at lethal range from it almost impossible.

Airborne depth-charges were therefore now given a 50-foot depth setting. Though this increased the fear in which aircraft were held by U-boats, it was still too deep for any high probability of inflicting lethal damage. Work was, therefore, begun on producing a 25-foot setting, which was, in combination with the Leigh Light and improved radar (to come in time), to make the aircraft a very deadly opponent of the U-boat. The Leigh Light, which was to make even the darkest night unsafe for a U-boat on the surface, and the new centimetric radar, which was for the first time to make it possible, in aircraft and escort vessels, to detect a surfaced submarine at night at a range greater than that of the human eye, were things of the future; but they were being actively developed and tested at this time. The time was approaching, therefore, when the well-trained and fully-equipped escort vessel would be able to account itself more than a match for the U-boat. The pendulum was swinging in favour of the surface craft. Before this ascendancy was established, however, there were to be some fierce battles in which losses were suffered on both sides.

His submarines' lack of success in the Western Approaches during July and August, 1941, led Admiral Dönitz to send them once again westwards towards Greenland, seeking as always for a weak spot where they need not be for ever searching the skies for enemy aircraft and where they need not face the increasingly well-organised escort groups. In September they found it. The end-to-end escort of trans-Atlantic convoys which had been adopted had been the principal cause for the U-boats eastward move which had proved so unprofitable. It had not, however, been the strength of the escort in the western part of the convoy route that had forced this move but the failure to locate the convoys themselves.

Dönitz now reconsidered the problem and concluded that his patrol lines had been wrongly stationed. To take the best advantage of the air and surface escorts stationed in Iceland, the convoys had been taking an extreme northerly route. A strong force of 17 boats was now spread between the coasts of Iceland and Greenland. On the 9th September they were rewarded by a signal from one of their number that a very large convoy weakly escorted was in sight. The widely spread patrol line was called in and one by one arrived on the scene, to find themselves confronted with the sort of rich prize they had been vainly seeking since the end of the 'Happy Time'.

Convoy SC42 had sailed from Sydney, Cape Breton, on the 30th August, 1941. Its 65 ships had been formed up in 12 columns under the local escort of three corvettes of the Royal Canadian Navy. The broad pendant of Commodore W. B. Mackenzie, R.N.R., flew from the masthead of the freighter *Everleigh*. A thirteenth column of five more ships from St. John's, Newfoundland, joined off that port on the 2nd September. At the same time the local escort was replaced for the ocean passage by the 24th Escort Group, comprising the destroyer H.M.C.S. *Skeena* and three Canadian corvettes, *Alberni, Kenogami* and *Orillia*. The senior officer of the escort was Commander J. C. Hibbard, R.C.N., of the *Skeena*.

The Royal Canadian Navy had grown from the squadron of 12 little ships with which it had entered the war so that numerically it was now strong enough to take over the escort of convoys in the comparatively safe waters of the Western Atlantic. The Royal Navy, over-extended in every ocean, had gladly delegated these duties to its Canadian comrades. National pride had demanded that Canadian ships should be formed into wholly Canadian groups; but herein lay a weakness. Little warships of the corvette class could be built and equipped more rapidly than crews to man them could be properly trained. Though the lesson that ill-trained escorts were no match for U-boats had been learnt from harsh experience, the relative quiet on the western portion of the convoy route during the summer had made it seem a fair risk to employ newly commissioned ships and weak, newly formed groups in that area.

In the case of SC42 the group commander was an experienced and skilful destroyer captain. His ship *Skeena* was a well-equipped and fairly modern destroyer like the 'A-I' class of the Royal Navy. The three corvettes, on the other hand, had been recently commissioned, their crews hastily trained, and sent to sea lacking experience. As in the early days of the campaign on the other side of the Atlantic, though Commander Hibbard's flotilla had been given the title, 24th Escort Group, in truth it still only comprised four ships fortuitously thrown together. Reporting on the events about to be described, Hibbard was to comment on this fact and that 'a far greater volume of signals was necessary than would ordinarily be the case where ships of an escort group know and understand the senior officer of the escort's intentions'. It is against such a background that the battle around SC42 must be viewed.

For the first four days after the convoy rounded Cape Race and headed north-eastwards towards distant Iceland, easterly gales and heavy seas buffeted the deeply laden freighters. The convoy's nominal speed of $7\frac{1}{2}$ knots could not be kept up. By the 5th September it was hove-to, the ships barely keeping steerage way on them. So they remained for two days. When the wind at last began to take off a little on the 7th and the slow progress resumed, Hibbard was relieved to find that, but for a detached group of five ships being shepherded by the *Kenogami*, 10 miles to the northward, his convoy was still complete. On the other hand, when a break in the overcast enabled him to fix his position by sun-sights, he calculated that only 3 knots had been made good during the last four days. A signal, reporting that he would be 72 hours late at the Western Ocean Meeting Point, was sent off for the benefit of the escorts from Iceland which would be coming to meet him.

Meanwhile, in the U-boat tracking room in the Admiralty, intercepted signals from U-boats had betrayed the fact that a group of them was gathering, barring the direct route to the predetermined meeting point. A diversion of course, at sunset on the 8th September, was ordered. The new route led due north up the coast of Greenland. It was hoped that this would take the convoy in a wide sweep round the submarine patrol line. It was of no avail. Early the following morning, 9th September, the S.S. *Jedmore,* straggling somewhat astern, raised the first alarm as a periscope was sighted and the tracks of two torpedoes passed close ahead of her. The escorts converged on the area and for 45 minutes probed unsuccessfully with their asdics. Then the *Orillia* was sent to search for five miles astern before rejoining. Kept down for a time by these manœuvres, the U-boat dropped far behind. She could not get to an attacking position again without making a long circuitous advance beyond the horizon. But before attacking, the signal which reported the convoy's position had been made to U-boat Command and had been picked up by the 16 other boats on the patrol line. At once they turned to intercept, their tedious scanning of an empty and stormy ocean at an end.

By midnight several had gathered round. For the next 30 hours confusion and dismay reigned in the convoy. The first ship to be torpedoed was the S.S. *Muneric*, loaded with iron ore, fourth ship of the port column. With such a cargo, she went quickly to the bottom. Hibbard took *Skeena* racing round in a wide circle from her station ahead of the convoy to search down the port side of the convoy. By the light of her starshells, the *Kenogami* sighted the submarine responsible, reported it to the escort commander and turned in chase. The U-boat dived but the corvette could get no contact by asdic. Eager to bring his more experienced asdic team into action, but ignorant of *Kenogami*'s position, Hibbard, over the radio-telephone, ordered her to fire starshells to guide him or to show a light. He was unaware that the corvette carried no starshell. No guiding light had been seen when rockets soaring up from the convoy called for Hibbard's attention elsewhere. Instructing *Kenogami* to continue to search for ten minutes, and, if no contact was gained, to rejoin the convoy, picking up survivors on the way, he hurried back.

From the Commodore, Hibbard learnt that a second U-boat had been sighted. With his meagre force of slow escorts, his own, faster ship restricted in speed by a shortage of fuel consequent on the three days' delay caused by the storm, the problem of giving the convoy adequate cover was insoluble. Its front stretched across more than six sea-miles. It was over three miles in length. Hibbard could only pray for luck to bring him an enemy in his path, when perhaps he could avenge those he could not protect.

Shortly before 3 a.m. from rockets, lights and machine-gun fire he learnt that a U-boat had been sighted amongst the columns of ships. Swinging his destroyer round he took her down between the seventh and eighth columns. As he did so, the Commodore ordered an emergency turn of all ships together 45 degrees to port. Nightmare manœuvres followed as the *Skeena* weaved her way through the great concourse of darkened ships, constant calls for full speed ahead or astern being necessary to avoid collision. In the midst of it all, a ship blew up as a torpedo struck home. Four minutes later two other explosions occurred, one in a ship right alongside the *Skeena*. Tracer bullets streaming out from several ships guided Hibbard to the U-boat. As *Skeena* passed closely across the bow of a ship in the seventh column, he saw her. A tight turn round the stern of another ship, his turbines screaming and his bridge structure rattling as every ounce of power wrenched the destroyer round, brought him in position to ram.

It was too late. The U-boat had dived. In the confused water of the criss-crossing ships' wakes, and the rough seas, his asdic could distinguish no contact. Not until the merchant ships had drawn a safe distance away could he drop depth charges, hopefully, at random and in vain.

As the convoy steamed slowly onward, Hibbard could do nothing but hasten after it himself, and detail the *Orillia* to sweep astern and, if no contact resulted, to pick up survivors, while he exhorted the other two corvettes, of whose position he was ignorant, to rejoin with all speed. That at least three U-boats were engaged was evident. It was perhaps as well that it was not realised that no less than 17 were closing in on the almost defenceless convoy. The temptation to order the ships to scatter might have been too strong. A worse disaster might then have occurred as ships were picked off one by one. It was to be bad enough.

Soon after 4 a.m. *Skeena* was back in her screening position. A brief lull followed; but at 5.10 the now familiar thud of an exploding torpedo signalled a renewal of the attack. While *Skeena* vainly fired her questing starshell, another ship was hit half an hour later. A ship on the starboard side signalling that a submarine was in sight, Commodore Mackenzie ordered once again an emergency turn away to port. It had little effect as torpedo after torpedo got home, distress rockets sending their despairing messages into the sky. As the alarm died away, *Kenogami* and *Alberni* dropped back to rescue the crews of the torpedoed ships. In so desperate a situation it is hard to say what else they could have done; but the convoy was bereft of all protection except *Skeena*. The *Orillia*, far astern of the convoy since the previous attack, had made a peculiar signal: 'Am complying with your orders. Request to remain until daylight. Have good reasons.' Distracted by the dire events going on around him, the escort commander replied, 'Approved. Report situation at daylight and then rejoin.' Thus a quarter of his force was dispensed with. And in fact Hibbard was to hear no more of *Orillia* until five days later when he learnt that she had arrived at Reykyavik, escorting a damaged tanker which she had towed part of the way.

Meanwhile the 10th of September had dawned to reveal the convoy still punching into heavy seas at a mere 5 knots. Only *Skeena* was in her station ahead. *Alberni* and *Kenogami* were coming up from astern, their mess-decks and cabins crowded with survivors, when the leading ship of the second column from port, the CAM-ship *Empire Hudson*, was torpedoed at 8 a.m. Sweeping down the port side of the convoy, *Skeena* gained asdic contact with, apparently, a submarine, and attacked. The satisfaction of being able to hit back at his persistent and seemingly ubiquitous enemy was short lived as Hibbard received a signal from the Commodore that a periscope had been sighted passing ahead of his ship. *Skeena* hurried back to the convoy, to try to ward off yet another attack evidently impending.

It failed to materialise. For the next four hours no attack developed though at 1 p.m. a burst of machine-gun firing at a periscope by ships of the port column sent the convoy side-stepping in an emergency turn to starboard. *Skeena* raced to the spot and scattered depth-charges but could get no contact with the submarine. Barely had she got back to her station when at 2.45 p.m. the leading ship of the ninth column was torpedoed. Calling his two corvettes to join him Hibbard took the three ships spread out in a line to search round the probable position from which the submarine had fired. As they were doing so, ships in the rear of the convoy opened fire at some object in the water astern of them. The escorts swung back. Ahead of them was a periscope which remained impudently in view surveying the scene for nearly a minute. A quick attack by eye made by the *Skeena* was followed by others on an asdic contact. A huge air bubble bursting on the surface after her last attack, followed by loss of all contact, convinced Hibbard that at last revenge had been taken on one of the enemy. The corvettes were sent back to the convoy while *Skeena* remained for an hour probing with her asdic.

No further sign of the U-boat was picked up, though asdic conditions were seemingly excellent. By 5.30 p.m. *Skeena* was back in her station, her crew soberly confident that a U-boat had been sent to the bottom. Post-war records, however, fail to confirm this. As was to be shown on many occasions, strange water disturbances and even explosions, believed to indicate the destruction of a submarine, proved not to do so. The Admiralty was very right to demand more concrete evidence before recording a 'kill'.

For the remainder of that day, the 10th September, the convoy enjoyed a respite. At dusk Commodore Mackenzie wheeled the great rectangle of ships round to a north-easterly course. Speed had picked up a little as the seas gradually diminished, though it was still a mere 6 knots. The following day a strong escort force from Iceland was due to join. Another small reinforcement of two Canadian corvettes which had been on a training cruise was also heading for the convoy and would arrive during the night.

Before this could happen, a few minutes after midnight, the now all too familiar routine of explosions, rockets and starshells began again. As the convoy swung away in an emergency turn a submarine on the surface was reported by the leader of Column Eight. Indeed by now the U-boats, having taken the measure of the weak opposition to be expected, were behaving with increasing boldness. During the next two hours, three were sighted in the convoy as they coolly picked their targets. The exhausted escorts, which had been continuously in action for 24 hours, cast back and forth searching for their tormentors without result until, at 2.15 a.m., from the *Kenogami* was seen a low, black silhouette barely 500 yards away on her port bow. It was so close that her single 4-inch gun could not be depressed sufficiently to hit. Then the U-boat dived. The asdic picked up the target and a pattern of 10 depth-charges was sent down towards it. But this submarine was also to escape. Three more ships had been torpedoed. The order to rejoin the convoy came through before further depth-charge attacks could be made. The sea was littered with boats and rafts from which survivors of two sunken ships were picked up on the way.

While all this was taking place, however, yet another U-boat, waiting ahead of the convoy as it approached, was paying the penalty of over-confidence. Unnoticed by the exultant look-outs, from another direction two bluff, chunky little craft were drawing near at their best speed of 16 knots.

The Canadian corvettes *Chambly* and *Moosejaw* had not long been in commission, but they were nearing the end of an intensive period of training and 'work-up'. They were commanded by J. D. Prentice, a retired Commander of the Royal Navy, lent, with a team of Royal Navy asdic operators, to the Royal Canadian Navy. On the 5th September, they had been lying in the harbour of St. John's, scheduled to sail on a training cruise on the 9th. A study of the U-boat dispositions promulgated by the Admiralty convinced Prentice that SC42 was likely to be intercepted. His training might therefore be given a more practical slant if he took his two ships in support. Permission was sought and obtained. At noon *Chambly* and *Moosejaw* passed between the iron-bound cliffs flanking the harbour entrance and steered to the north-east.

Having got well ahead of SC42, Prentice passed the 7th, 8th and 9th, putting his corvettes through simple exercises and manœuvres, shaping his predominantly landsmen crews into seamen. Then, at 2.15 in the morning of the 10th September, the message he had been expecting was handed to him. 'A ship of SC42 has been attacked. Proceed with dispatch to join and escort convoy to Iceland if fuel permits. Steer to reach position ahead of convoy.' Thus it was that at midnight that day, as he steered westwards at his best speed, rockets from SC42 to the southward told him that his little force was to have its first experience of real action. Turning southwards he saw more rockets at 13 minutes after midnight, and again 22 minutes later.

At that moment, on the bridge of the *Chambly*, Prentice heard the asdic operator, Leading Seaman A. H. Johnson of his training team, shout 'Contact-Red Nine-O'. The clear-cut echo he could hear coming from the loud-speaker and Johnson's confident assessment of it as a submarine, only 700 yards away, brooked of no delay in taking action. A spatter of orders went to the helmsman and to the depth-charge team on the quarter deck, as *Chambly* was brought round on to an attack course, with weapons at the ready. Directed by a young Canadian, Sub-Lieutenant Chenoweth, R.C.N.V.R., who had just joined the ship and was on his first trip to sea, a pattern of five depth-charges was fired. As the explosions set the *Chambly* shuddering and leaping in the water, Prentice turned her back to repeat the attack. *Moosejaw* was already running in to do so when, with a swirl and a cascade of white water frothing off its casings, *U501* rose to the surface close ahead of her. *Moosejaw*'s searchlight stabbed out and settled on the submarine's conning-tower. A single round from the corvette's 4-inch gun slammed a shell into it. Before more could be fired the *Moosejaw* had collided with the U-boat which was still going slowly ahead. Before the two vessels sheered apart again, a single figure made a wild leap from the U-boat's bridge on to the corvette's deck. It proved to be *U501*'s captain.

The remainder of the German crew had by now mustered on the deck of the submarine. Most of them leapt into the water and were picked up by *Moosejaw*. Meanwhile Prentice had taken *Chambly* alongside the U-boat with the intention of boarding and, if possible, capturing her. He found that the diesel engines were still running and sending her through the water at some three to four knots. Hailing the men on deck he ordered them to stop the engines or they would not be rescued. This had the desired effect and *Chambly*'s boarding party were soon on their way in the corvette's boat. Awkwardly they scrambled aboard. Before they could make their way down through the conning-tower hatch, however, it became clear that the submarine was sinking. As British and Germans abandoned her together, the First Lieutenant of *Chambly*, in charge of the boarding party, was sucked down, narrowly escaping drowning. His experience gave the clue to the disappearance of one man from *Chambly*, Stoker Brown, who must have lost his life in the same way.

The destruction of *U501* was a remarkable outcome of a 'training cruise'. It was a piece of beginner's luck, perhaps. It was certainly cause for envy by the disheartened escort of SC42, frustrated in their efforts to hit back at the enemy by the necessity to rescue the crews of torpedoed ships and the inability to devote much time to offensive action before hurrying back to the defenceless convoy. Careful and conscientious training must also be credited to Prentice's success. *Kenogami*, for example, had three times had U-boats in sight at close range, but her inexperienced team had been unable to take advantage of it. In contrast stood out the instant, sure classification of contact by *Chambly*'s asdic team, the prompt action by Prentice himself and the accurate attack which brought *U501* to the surface in surrender.

Meanwhile SC42's agony was by no means halted by this single success. Three ships had been torpedoed at about the time *Chambly* and *Moosejaw* joined the escort at 3.30 a.m. An hour and a half later two more went to the bottom. No sight of the enemy was obtained. With only three escorts to cover the straggling convoy—*Kenogami* and *Alberni* were far astern picking up survivors—this was not to be wondered at. At daylight Hibbard counted his charges and found that no less than 20 were missing. Of these 15 had been sunk. It was with heartfelt relief, therefore, that during the forenoon of the 11th reinforcements joined, the corvettes *Wetaskiwin* (Canadian), *Mimosa* (Free French) and *Gladiolus* (British) and the trawler H.M.S. *Buttermere*. Soon after midday a more substantial reinforcement arrived, the 2nd Escort Group from Iceland, comprising the destroyers *Douglas, Veteran, Saladin, Skate* and *Leamington*, the senior officer being Commander W. E. Banks in the *Douglas*.

Hibbard must have envied Banks his abundance of fast escorts as he thankfully and wearily vacated his position as senior officer. Banks was able to throw out a hunting force, comprising *Veteran* and *Leamington,* to search for and keep down any submarines hovering beyond the horizon. Furthermore SC42 was now within range of aircraft operating from Iceland. It was from one of them that the first report of the enemy came. A U-boat was sighted on the surface 15 miles ahead of the convoy. *Veteran* and *Leamington* were well placed and were sent scurrying away to hunt. Half an hour later *Veteran* reported a submarine in sight on the surface. Banks sent *Saladin* and *Skate* away in support. They were not needed, however. In *Veteran* and *Leamington*—the latter one of the ex-American 'four-stackers'—well-drilled anti-submarine teams went into action. At dusk the four ships rejoined bringing the welcome news that the U-boat had been certainly destroyed. It was in fact *U207*.

Through that night, for the first time since the attack had started on the 9th September, the convoy steamed on unmolested. The watch below, in escorts and merchantmen alike, were able to sleep undisturbed by the clang of the alarm bell. As a quiet day followed and another undisturbed night, taut nerves relaxed, and the strain went out of eyes which for three nights and days had ceaselessly scanned the surface of the sea around them for the low, sinister shape of the lurking enemy, the sly, prying eye of a periscope or the dreaded streak of an approaching torpedo.

German records say that but for foggy weather the attack would have been renewed. It is true that five of the U-boat pack continued to trail SC42 and that during the night of the 16th September, the last night before the convoy reached safe waters in the Minches, one more ship straggling astern was torpedoed to bring the total score of losses to 16. But it is unlikely that any determined attack would have been made in the face of the strong sea and air escort provided. This included, for a few hours on the 14th September, three United States Navy destroyers, an early instance of America's participation in the Battle of the Atlantic even before she was officially at war.

The long-drawn battle round SC42 had exposed a serious weakness in the Atlantic life-line. Though end-to-end escort of convoys had been instituted, the protection given in the western part of their voyages was inadequate in size and quality. In spite of the steady increase in the number of escorts available, this could not yet be overcome. It lacked, too, the essential air cover, as the existing gap was unbridgeable by the type of aircraft in use. Fortunately for the Allied cause, many of the U-boats which had intercepted SC42 had expended most of their torpedoes and were short of fuel by the end of the battle. They returned to base leaving only five to reform the patrol line off Greenland. These intercepted SC44. They sank four merchant ships and the Canadian corvette *Levis* before they, too, had to turn for home.

It seemed to the U-boat Command that at last a chance to renew earlier success was at hand, by striking before the western gap in the convoy defences could be bridged. It was not to be. For some time Hitler had been pressing his Naval Staff to send U-boats to the Mediterranean which he considered was 'the decisive area for the future conduct of the war'. Admiral Dönitz, never wavering in his belief that by attack on her merchant shipping in the Atlantic

1 *Admiral Karl Dönitz, Commander-in-Chief of the German U-boat fleet throughout the Battle of the Atlantic*

2 *Admiral Sir Percy Noble, G.B.E., K.C.B., C.V.O., the architect of victory in the Atlantic*

3 *Admiral Sir Max Horton, K.C.B., D.S.O., Commander-in-Chief, Western Approaches, from November 1942 to the end of the war*

5   *U-boat on patrol in the Atlantic*

6 *Otto Kretschmer, top-scoring U-boat commander. Captured with his crew when U99 was destroyed in March 1941*

7 *Joachim Schepke: one of the early aces. Lost with U100 in March 1941*

8 *Günther Prien, who sank the 'Royal Oak' at Scapa Flow. An outstanding commander in the Battle of the Atlantic, Prien was lost with U47 in March 1941*

U-BOAT COMMANDERS

9 Black Swan-class frigate of the escort forces

10 H.M.S. 'Hesperus', an escort-force destroyer—the principal U-boat killers—entering harbour after ramming and sinking U357

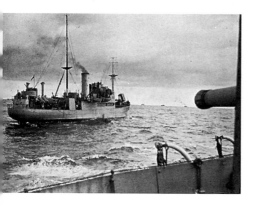

11 A rescue ship. Its task of picking up survivors from torpedoed ships astern of the convoys called for courage and seamanship of a high order

12 *Flower-class corvette: mainstay of the escort forces for most of the Battle of the Atlantic*

13 *Deep-sea trawler of the escort forces*

14 *River-class frigate*

15 *Ex-American destroyer at the capture of a U-boat*

16 *U-boat in an Atlantic gale*

17 *One of the smaller Atlantic convoys*

18 *U-boat's conning-tower*

19 *Escort's bridge*

20 (top) *Surface-raider's victim*

21 (centre) *Torpedoed tanker*

22 (bottom) *Torpedoed while in convoy*

23 (top) *Another tanker*

24 (centre) *American freighter*

25 (bottom) *Sunk by the 'Scharnhorst'*

26 *U-boat surrenders*

27 (left) *Lieutenant-Commander (now Rear-Admiral) Peter Gretton, D.S.O., O.B.E., D.S.C., Royal Navy, an outstanding escort-group commander*

28 *Captain F. J. Walker, C.B., D.S.O., Royal Navy, the most successful U-boat hunter of the Second World War*

29 *Hurricane launched from a Catapult Aircraft Merchant-ship (CAM-ship)*

30 *Escort-carrier 'Biter': one of the first to bridge the 'black gap' in the convoy air cover*

31 *Escort-carrier with convoy*

33 *The Attacker:*
U-boat captain at
the periscope

34 *The Attacked: U-boat crew await*
depth-charge explosions

35 *By a Focke-Wulf 200 Kondor long-range bomber*

36 *By a Stuka dive-bomber*

AIR ATTACK ON CONVOYS

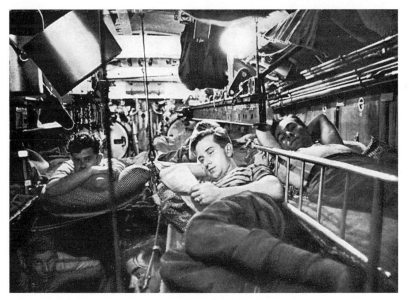

39, 40 *Life in an operational U-boat*

41–44 (overleaf) *Survivors from torpedoed merchantmen*

45 *U-boat's engine room*

48 *Depth-charge explodes*

49 *Re-loading depth-charge throwers in a rough sea*

50   *Liberator*

51   (left)   *Sunderland*

52   *Focke-Wulf 200*

53   *Swordfish*

54 *Convoy-protection Operations Room*

his U-boats could bring Britain to her knees, had resisted this policy through the summer months. Now he was to be overborne. At the moment when a fresh chance to strike a crippling blow had come, the means with which to deal it was snatched from his hand.

7

A Notable Defeat of the Wolf-Packs

THE INTERDEPENDENCE of the several theatres of war and the crucial effect of sea-power in each was clearly demonstrated by the naval strategy forced on the Germans at this time. In the Mediterranean the successful maintenance of Malta as a base for operations, as a result of the achievements of Sir James Somerville's Force 'H', based on Gibraltar, and of the Mediterranean Fleet from Alexandria, under Sir Andrew Cunningham, in running supply convoys and carrier-borne air reinforcements through to it, had become intolerable to the Germans. The position of Rommel's Afrika Korps, dependent upon sea-borne supplies from Italy, was undermined by the severe losses being inflicted on convoys running between Sicily and North Africa.

Since the Italian Navy and Air Force were unable to wrest control of the Central Basin of the Mediterranean from the British, it became necessary for the Germans to take a hand. When orders reached the U-boat Command for, first, six and, later, four more submarines to be sent through the Straits of Gibraltar, Admiral Dönitz accepted this reduction of his striking power in the Atlantic, concurring in the strategical necessity for it. The sinking of the *Ark Royal* and *Barham* in November 1941 and of the cruiser *Galatea* a month later seemed certainly a worth-while dividend. But when, on the 22nd November, 1941, Dönitz received orders for the transfer of the entire force of operational U-boats to the Mediterranean and the approaches to the Straits of Gibraltar, he clearly saw the strategic mistake which was being made. In his *Memoirs* he has stated his convictions, with which British naval opinion will not disagree:

> The most important task of the German Navy, and therefore of the German U-boat arm, and the task which over-shadowed in importance everything else, was the conduct of operations against shipping on Britain's vital lines of communication across the Atlantic. . . .
>
> The number of U-boats transferred to the Mediterranean should have been kept down to a minimum, and to have denuded the Atlantic as we did and put an end to all operations there for something like seven weeks was, in my opinion, completely unjustifiable.

In his official history, *The War at Sea*, Captain Roskill states the British view:

> Not only did the German U-boats suffer considerable losses in their new theatre—no less than seven were sunk in November and December —but their transfer from the Atlantic brought us a welcome easement in that vital theatre.

It was, in truth, a 'welcome easement'. No means existed of repairing the weak link in the convoy defences in the Western Atlantic, betrayed by the disastrous passage of SC42 in September. For convoys on other routes had been under heavy attack also. In the same month a small convoy of 11 ships homeward-bound from Freetown—SL87—was located by a U-boat on the 23rd, far out in the Atlantic. Three other U-boats were called in to the attack. Owing to the length of this route, only escorts with considerable endurance could be employed on it. Few were available. Those there were sacrificed in speed what they gained in endurance. Thus, SL87's escort comprised the old sloop *Bideford*, the *Gorleston*, one of the ex-American coastguard cutters acquired under lend-lease, the corvette *Gardenia* and a diminutive Free French vessel, *Commandant Duboc*. Once again, a mixed force, unused to working together. The result was a foregone conclusion. Attacked on three successive nights, only four ships of the convoy remained when daylight on the fourth day came.

The Gibraltar convoys were potentially the most vulnerable of all, passing as they did within easy reach of the German U-boat bases on the Biscay coast, and of the airfield near Bordeaux, whence the F.-W. Kondors operated. Being made up for the most part of small freighters engaged in the Spanish trade, and escorted through-out their voyage, they had not up to now attracted the same attention as the more important and, at first, less well-protected trans-Atlantic traffic. But with the increase in the number of operational U-boats available, the improvement in efficiency of the Focke-Wulf aircraft co-operating with them and the stiff opposition encountered else-where, they were now to come under more frequent attack. Here, too, the route was a long one, and, though destroyers of the local flotilla at Gibraltar could be sent out to augment the escort for the last few days of the passage, it was not possible for the old destroyers of the Western Approaches Command to accompany them for the whole journey. Thus, as on the Freetown route, sloops and corvettes made up the escort.

Not only was their speed inadequate in opposition to the U-boats, but they were virtually helpless in face of the bombing attacks of the F.-W. Kondors. Against the latter, as has been mentioned in the previous chapter, fighter-catapult-ships and CAM-ships had been fitted out. They had a moderate success. But it was the auxiliary aircraft-carrier which was to provide convoys with the continuous air cover which was to be one of the decisive developments in the Battle of the Atlantic. The first of these was *Audacity*, com-manded by Commander D. W. Mackendrick. Intended primarily to provide fighter cover, she was equipped only with Grumman 'Martlet' fighters. Successful as these were in keeping the Focke-Wulfs at a distance, they also quickly demonstrated their value in detecting shadowing submarines or those running on the surface, in order to attain attacking positions ahead of the convoy. They could then force them to submerge, meanwhile calling out escort craft to hunt them. On the other hand, until anti-submarine aircraft, capable of carrying their own under-water weapons, were embarked, the slow escorts allotted to the Gibraltar convoys could not be got to the scene with any good chance of gaining contact with the enemy.

It was with a convoy outward-bound for Gibraltar, OG74, with an escort of a sloop and five Flower-class corvettes, that *Audacity* sailed on 13th September, 1941, on her first escort duty. OG74 comprised 27 merchantmen, mostly small freighters normally en-gaged in the Spanish trade, and the Ocean Boarding Vessel H.M.S.

Corinthian, en route to her patrol station in the South Atlantic. The routine followed by Commander Mackendrick was to take *Audacity* clear of the convoy each evening at dusk and to rejoin each morning. Throughout daylight hours a patrol of two Martlets was kept in the air. On the evening of the 15th September they had their first sight of the enemy, when a U-boat was surprised on the surface just over the horizon from the convoy and on its port bow. The U-boat hastily dived without having gained a sight of the convoy. On receipt of the report from the aircraft, the senior officer of the escort, Lieutenant-Commander H. R. White in the *Deptford*, despatched one of his corvettes, the *Pentstemon*. At her best speed it was still more than an hour before she could reach the diving position of the submarine. By that time her quarry could be anywhere inside a circle covering 80 square miles. When *Pentstemon* rejoined the convoy in the early hours of the 16th she had no contact to report; but the U-boat had been kept down, ignorant of the passage of the convoy, which thereby gained three days' respite.

It was not through enemy action that the convoy suffered its first casualty. In the dark hour before dawn two of the merchant ships came into collision, one of them, the *City of Waterford*, being sunk. This was one of the few occasions during the war when the natural hazards of steaming unhandy merchantmen in close formation led to such fatal results.

Not until the 20th September was the convoy located by the enemy when an outward-bound U-boat came across it by chance. Signalling its position to the U-boat Command, the submarine settled down to shadow it from just beyond the horizon. Here she was discovered by one of *Audacity*'s aircraft during the afternoon. Calling for the corvette *Arbutus* to join him, the senior officer of the escort took the *Deptford* away to the attack. An asdic contact an hour later was held and attacked repeatedly but without any evidence of success. When two destroyers on anti-submarine patrol arrived on the scene, *Deptford* and *Arbutus* left to rejoin the convoy. As they were doing so, starshells blossoming in the sky ahead announced that another submarine, directed to the scene as a result of the first U-boat's signals, had attacked. A signal from *Pentstemon* gave the news that two freighters had been torpedoed, that a third, the

Walmer Castle, was picking up survivors and that the convoy had scattered. This last statement was not true. But daylight on the 21st September certainly revealed a reduction in the number of ships present. Besides the *Walmer Castle*, left behind carrying out her mission of rescue, and the two ships known to have been sunk, four others were missing. These had not, in fact, deliberately broken convoy, but in the confusion of the night attack they had missed or misunderstood the Commodore's signal for an emergency turn. In the darkness they had lost touch and at daylight found themselves in an isolated group out of sight of the main body.

With daylight a new threat to the convoy arrived in the shape of a Focke-Wulf Kondor. Coming across the unprotected *Walmer Castle*, the aircraft bombed her, set her on fire and left her in a sinking condition. When the *Deptford* and *Marigold* got back to her there was nothing left for them to do but to pick up the survivors. Revenge was taken, however, when a Martlet scored *Audacity*'s first concrete success by shooting down the enemy aircraft into the sea. This rid the convoy of the somewhat demoralising and previously inescapable enemy aircraft circling endlessly on the horizon and calling the U-boats in to the attack. Nevertheless, there was to be one more misfortune to OG74 before it could shake off its attackers. Through the darkness distress flares were sighted. Coming up to them, the *Deptford* and *Marigold* found rafts to which were clinging seven men, all that were left of the crew of the freighter *Runa*, one of the four ships which had lost touch with the convoy the previous night.

This was the final loss suffered by convoy OG74. Five ships out of 27 had gone. It was a minor calamity in comparison with some others, but the impunity with which the two U-boats involved had taken their toll betrayed the weakness of a surface escort composed only of slow sloops and corvettes gathered haphazardly together. Two things combined to prevent an even greater loss—the presence of *Audacity* with her ubiquitous patrolling aircraft and the location by the enemy of a more worthwhile target in the shape of a homeward-bound convoy, HG73. This had a numerically stronger escort—a sloop and eight corvettes. On the other hand it had no air cover and no fast escorts. As had been proved over and over again, the resultant reduction of the escorts to a purely passive, defensive role gave the attackers an overwhelming advantage. The outcome was disastrous. Out of 27 ships forming the convoy, nine were torpedoed and sunk in three successive night attacks by four U-boats.

These successful attacks on the Sierra Leone and Gibraltar convoys, in the same month as occurred the decimation of SC42 in the western Atlantic, were a severe blow. They had both been escorted by numerically strong surface escorts. One of them had enjoyed the additional protection of the auxiliary aircraft-carrier *Audacity*. The escorts themselves had for the most part had the benefit of an intensive training at the base set up at Tobermory in the Isle of Mull, H.M.S. *Western Isles*, under the command of Commodore G. O. Stephenson, Vice-Admiral, Retired. Yet U-boats had penetrated their defensive screen with complete impunity to sink merchantmen in the convoys. Something was obviously wrong. Lack of any fast ships—destroyers—to take advantage of the occasions when U-boats were sighted on the surface certainly robbed the escort of offensive capacity and allowed the enemy to gain ideal attacking positions. But there was more to it than that.

In the absence of an efficient radar—the first 10-centimetre wavelength set was in production, but was not yet fitted in any escorts—logically worked out and concerted effort by all the escorts simultaneously was necessary to ensure bringing an attacking submarine within detection range of one of them. For this a high standard of team training was necessary. The need for such training and for keeping escort groups, so trained, together under a familiar commander had been early recognised by those closest to the problem; but the implementation of it had been often frustrated by the shifting nature and requirements of the wide-spread campaign. A threat to a particular convoy or to convoys on one particular route often called for reinforcements to be gathered from where they could be found. Whereas regularly constituted escort groups had been allocated to the route of paramount importance, that which led to and from America, escorts for the less vital Gibraltar convoys had often been formed of 'scratch' teams gathered for the occasion. When, as a result of the German re-deployment of their U-boat fleet to the Mediterranean and into the approaches to the Straits of

Gibraltar, the black pins on the map in the U-boat tracking room at the Admiralty showed the increasing threat to the Gibraltar convoys, steps to improve the quality of the escorts on that route were taken. One of the escort groups whose organisation was tightened up at this time was the 36th. To command it, in October 1941, was appointed an officer who was to become the best known and most successful group commander on the Allied side in the Battle of the Atlantic, though his principal exploits in the field of submarine killing were not to take place until after the period covered by this book.

Commander F. J. Walker, R.N., was an officer who had specialised in anti-submarine warfare in the years before the war. Something of a 'stormy petrel', his differences of opinion with those in authority over him had damaged his career. Passed over for promotion to Captain, his talents had been wasted in uninspiring shore appointments during the first two years of the war. Now, however, he was given command of the sloop *Stork* and of the 36th Escort Group. The *Stork*, a product of the building programmes of the immediate pre-war years, was a considerable improvement on the older sloops on whom much of the burden of convoy escort had up to now rested. She could make 19½ knots and, instead of the miserable armament of three or four 4-inch guns, she had six dual-purpose 4-inch guns in twin-mountings. The anti-aircraft capabilities of this class of ship had, up to this time, led to their employment in the North Sea. But now they were to join the Western Approaches Escort Force, where for the rest of the war they were to prove excellent anti-submarine ships.

Besides the *Stork*, the 36th Escort Group included the old sloop *Deptford* and seven Flower-class corvettes. Walker at once brought his long experience of anti-submarine warfare to improve the efficiency of his group, not only as individual ships but as a well-knit team. At the group's base at Liverpool the depth-charge handling crews were put through incessant drills at the depth-charge 'loader' which had been set up on shore, until they learnt to handle the awkward, swaying 500-lb. cylinders on a rolling deck, so that a second 'pattern' of charges could be got ready within ten seconds of the first being fired. In the ingenious Attack Teacher, where synthetic submarine hunts and depth-charge attacks could be carried out, the control teams—captains, anti-submarine control officers and asdic operators—spent long hours perfecting their techniques.

None of this was of any use, however, unless the submarine could be got within the very limited range of the asdic. Study of past convoy battles made it clear to Walker that only by pre-arranged, concerted moves of the escorts could this be ensured. Otherwise it was only by pure luck that contact was made. He devised, therefore, an operation of this sort to which he gave the name 'Buttercup'. It was the forerunner of a number of such, varying only in detail, intended to deal with the various situations which might arise. At the simple order 'Buttercup Starboard' (or Port, Astern, etc., according to the position from which the U-boat was believed to have fired its torpedoes), the escorts would come round to a pre-arranged heading, which would ensure the whole of the probable area being swept by asdic. It took repeated practice to achieve the desired effect. Walker took every opportunity to put his team through their paces. His enthusiasm and the fighting spirit which permeated him soon spread throughout his group. His captains became similarly inspired and were soon so in tune with their leader's notions that they were able to carry out his wishes unbidden.

This was the team which, early in December 1941, lay at Gibraltar, while in the Roads gathered the 32 ships which were to form Convoy HG76. By this time the re-deployment of Admiral Dönitz's U-boat fleet had been accomplished. The majority of his operational boats, withdrawn from the trans-Atlantic routes, were now in the Mediterranean or athwart the approaches to the Straits of Gibraltar. Of the latter, seven were on their station. This was known to the Admiralty. A heavy attack on HG76 was certain. The convoy's sailing was therefore delayed until reinforcements for the 36th Escort Group could be gathered. By the 14th December, three destroyers, two sloops and three Flower-class corvettes became available to augment the normal escort, during the first two days of the convoy's passage when it would be breaking through the U-boat patrol line. During this time the convoy would also have the benefit of air escort by Naval Swordfish aircraft based ashore at Gibraltar. Thus for every two ships in the convoy there was an escort. In addition there was the auxiliary aircraft-carrier *Audacity*.

Though some of the reinforcements had left to return to Gibraltar before the ensuing convoy battle really began, it was certainly a most powerful escort, particularly when looked at in comparison with the meagre force of two or three sloops or corvettes which had often been expected to beat off wolf-pack attacks on other occasions. With the numbers available to him, Walker was able to station them in a double ring round the convoy, thus greatly increasing the difficulties of any U-boat trying to get through to attack the merchant ships. Nevertheless, numbers alone had been shown before to be not enough. Clear-sighted direction and trained crews were also needed. These the 36th Escort Group had. With them they were to achieve the outstanding success of this phase of the Battle of the Atlantic, before radar came to swing the pendulum to the side of the escorts.

On the afternoon of Sunday, the 14th December, the ships of HG76 filed out of Gibraltar Roads in the wake of the flagship of Commodore Raymond Fitzmaurice, the freighter *Spero*. By dark they were clear of the Straits and heading westwards out into the Atlantic in the usual rectangle made up of nine columns. From then onwards, as the Commodore was to report, 'the convoy had few dull moments'.

The first news of the enemy's presence came from the escorting Swordfish shortly before midnight. Running down a radar contact, the pilot sighted a U-boat lying in wait ahead of the convoy. Diving to the attack, he dropped his three depth-charges as the U-boat was submerging and marked the position with flares. The attack failed to put the submarine out of action; nor was the pilot able at once to get through to the *Stork* by radio. But hearing the explosions and sighting the flares, Walker steered for them and, with the sloop *Deptford* and the corvette *Rhododendron*, searched for some time. Though they were unsuccessful, the combined action of ships and aircraft kept the U-boat down and prevented an attack. It was no doubt the same submarine which the Swordfish encountered again two hours later, by that time well astern of the convoy. The aircraft had no depth-charges left but the U-boat was not to know this. It prudently submerged. The convoy steamed safely on into the night.

By daylight on the 15th, HG76 was beyond the operational radius of the aircraft from Gibraltar, but aircraft from *Audacity* took their place. As the little single-seater Martlets circled, nothing but empty sea met their pilots' eyes. Walker congratulated himself that the U-boats had been given the slip and concurred in the suggestion of Commander Mackendrick of *Audacity*, that, during the 16th December, the air patrols should be dispensed with, to conserve the flying hours of the four aircraft which were all that remained serviceable in the carrier. But in fact, though the U-boats had been temporarily shaken off, Dönitz's other arm, the Focke-Wulf Kondors, had regained contact with the convoy. One of them had been briefly sighted from the ex-American destroyer *Stanley* late on the 15th. The aircraft's signals set every U-boat in the area on to a course converging on the convoy.

They had a long way to come. Meanwhile the convoy steamed slowly on in fair, blue weather, at its best speed of $7\frac{1}{2}$ knots, while Commodore Fitzmaurice took advantage of the respite to drill his ships in making emergency turns (all ships turning together) and in wheels. In the afternoon of the 16th, five ships of the escort left to return to Gibraltar, but 12 remained. All was apparently quiet when darkness fell. But, unknown to the escort commander, a U-boat had arrived on the scene and, keeping out of sight beyond the horizon, had settled down to shadow while waiting for the wolf-pack to form up.

Her signals were picked up by Allied Direction-Finding Stations. During the night, signals went out to *Stork* warning the escort commander of impending attack. Before daylight, therefore, Walker got in touch with *Audacity* and asked Mackendrick to send out air patrols at dawn. Results were quickly forthcoming. Twenty-two miles on the port beam of the convoy a U-boat was discovered. On receipt of the aircraft's signals, Walker at once headed for the position at full speed, directing three destroyers, *Blankney*, *Exmoor* and *Stanley*, and the corvette *Pentstemon*—the three fastest of his ships and the nearest—to do the same. *Blankney* and *Exmoor* arriving first in the submarine's diving position, followed soon afterwards by *Stork*, Walker formed the three ships up for an organised search. While this was going on, *Pentstemon*, coming up to join the remainder in company with *Stanley*, made an asdic contact and attacked. Touch was then lost with her underwater target, so that, when orders came from *Stork* to join her unless in contact, *Stanley* and *Pentstemon* set course to do so. *Pentstemon* had wrought better than she knew, however, for some 90 minutes later a U-boat was sighted on the surface not far from her attack. Extensively damaged by the depth-charges, *U131* had been forced to surface. Walker's ships turned to engage, the destroyers *Exmoor* and *Blankney* quickly taking the lead. At the same time the fighter aircraft from *Audacity*, swooping down to machine-gun the U-boat bridge, was shot down and the pilot killed. Soon afterwards the submarine came under a concentrated and accurate gunfire to which only a feeble reply from her single gun could be made. With shells falling close around her, Baumann, her captain, realised the position was hopeless. He gave orders for *U131* to be scuttled. He and his whole crew were picked up by the *Exmoor* and *Stanley*.

This little action brought the convoy immunity for the remainder of the 17th December and, aided by an 80 degree alteration of course after dark, through the ensuing night also. It could not continue, though. Five other U-boats had been directed to HG76. They were closing in from every direction—none too confidently, for they had heard of the convoy's unusually powerful escort, and the flat calm and extreme visibility made it difficult to approach undetected.

It was the latter which brought about the next encounter. Korvetten-Kapitän Heyda, commanding *U434*, had been shadowing from the port quarter during the dark hours. As daylight grew, he left it too late to withdraw out of sight beyond the horizon. His boat was sighted, still on the surface, from the bridge of the *Stanley* at a range of six miles. Although *Stanley*'s asdic equipment was out of action owing to a defect, her captain, David Byam Shaw, swung her round and headed at full speed for the U-boat. When about three miles away it dived. While waiting for the arrival of the *Blankney*, coming to his assistance, Shaw circled the submarine, its position betrayed by an oil slick, and dropped single depth-charges. Then *Blankney* arrived, gained asdic contact and directed *Stanley* over the target to drop a pattern of 14 depth-charges. *Blankney* followed with another attack. Forty-nine minutes after being first sighted, *U434* came to the surface, her crew abandoned ship and she went to the bottom.

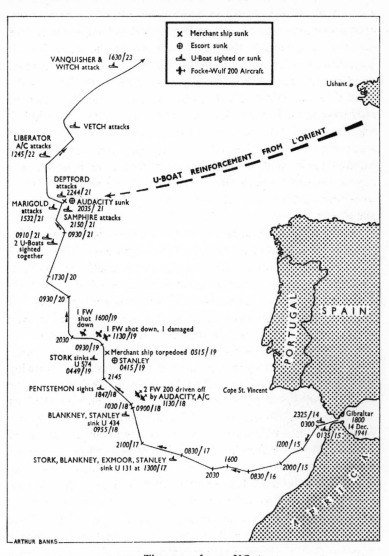

Legend:
- **X** Merchant ship sunk
- **⊕** Escort sunk
- **⚓** U-Boat sighted or sunk
- **✈** Focke-Wulf 200 Aircraft

VANQUISHER & WITCH attack — 1630/23

Ushant

VETCH attacks

LIBERATOR A/C attacks 1245/22

U-BOAT REINFORCEMENT FROM L'ORIENT

DEPTFORD attacks 2244/21

MARIGOLD attacks 1532/21

X ⊕ AUDACITY sunk 2035/21

SAMPHIRE attacks 2150/21

0910/21 — 0930/21 2 U-Boats sighted together

1730/20

0930/20

1 FW shot down 1600/19

1 FW shot down, 1 damaged 1130/19

2030

0930/19

X Merchant ship torpedoed 0515/19

STORK sinks U 574 0449/19

⊕ STANLEY 0415/19

2145

PENTSTEMON sights 1847/18

2 FW 200 driven off by AUDACITY, A/C 1130/18

1030/18 0900/18

BLANKNEY, STANLEY sink U 434 0955/18

Cape St. Vincent

2325/14

Gibraltar 1800 14 Dec. 1941

0300

0135/15

2100/17

0830/17

1200/15

STORK, BLANKNEY, EXMOOR, STANLEY sink U 131 at 1300/17

1600

2000/15

2030

0830/16

PORTUGAL

SPAIN

AFRICA

ARTHUR BANKS

32 *The passage of convoy HG76*
December 1941

These two successes were cause for considerable satisfaction to Commander Walker in his first encounter with the U-boat packs. Before even reaching a position from which to attack the convoy, two of the enemy had been hunted down and destroyed. There could be no complacency, however. It was known that others were somewhere around seeking for a gap in the defences, while Focke-Wulf Kondors made daily visits to reconnoitre the situation. But they were not able to linger, as was their wont, transmitting homing signals to the U-boats. Two that arrived during the forenoon of the 18th December were set upon by *Audacity*'s fighters and damaged before the Martlets' guns jammed.

Nevertheless, in the calm, clear weather in which the tip of a masthead or the smallest wisp of smoke showed up clearly against the sharp-cut horizon, the U-boats could hardly fail to locate the convoy. On the other hand, these conditions cut both ways. As dusk was falling on the 18th, the conning-tower of a submarine, surfacing in the last of the light, was sighted against the sunset glow from the *Pentstemon*. With *Convolvulus* and *Stanley* she turned in chase. Gunfire from *Pentstemon* forced the submarine to dive, but no asdic contact could be made and at 9.30 p.m., after two hours of fruitless search, the three ships set course to return to the convoy. With a persistence which, bearing in mind the strength of the opposition and the unfavourable conditions cannot but be admired, the submarine, *U574*, commanded by Korvetten-Kapitän Gentelbach, thereupon surfaced and followed the escorts towards the convoy. Thus it was that at 3.45 a.m., from her station astern of the convoy on the outer screen, *Stanley*'s radio-telephone crackled into life with the message 'Submarine in sight'. Then came a second message, 'Torpedoes passing from astern'.

It was a pitch-black night. Walker, in his station, also astern of the convoy, was uncertain of *Stanley*'s exact position. So that he could come to her aid, he ordered her to fire starshells to illuminate the submarine. Before she could do so, the two ships had come in sight of one another. They were exchanging identities by flash light when, in a blinding sheet of flame reaching hundreds of feet into the air, *Stanley* blew up. At this the whole convoy sprang into brilliant light. The merchant ships had been supplied with the 'Snowflake' rockets, introduced to deal with the problem of U-boats penetrating to between the columns. Instructed to fire them as soon as a ship was torpedoed, they now did so. The resultant naked exposure of the convoy was an uncomfortable experience. As the Commodore commented, 'One could not help being acutely aware that all ships of the convoy were vividly lighted up and shown to any other submarine that might be waiting to see their target. I do not know if "snowflake" illumination by convoy ships helped the escort—I doubt it.' Indeed this device, designed to deal with a particular situation rarely experienced, proved a two-edged weapon in practice and one hard to control. The introduction of an efficient radar set was soon to make it redundant. In this case its use must have been of assistance to the U-boat which was at that moment approaching from the convoy's port bow to put a torpedo into the leading ship of the port column, the S.S. *Ruckinge*.

In the meantime dramatic events were occurring astern of the convoy. On seeing *Stanley* torpedoed, Walker had ordered 'Buttercup Astern'. The escorts had turned to comply but it was in *Stork* herself that the ping of the asdic had suddenly returned the sharp echo which signified contact with a submarine. The range was very short —700 yards. There was no time for deliberation or careful aim. Walker took the *Stork* straight in for a snap attack before settling down to a deliberate hunt. But only one more depth-charge attack had been made and *Stork* was running in for a third time when *U574* surfaced 200 yards ahead of her. Walker steered to ram; but the U-boat set off in a tight circle at high speed. The *Stork* followed, unable at first to get inside the submarine's turning circle. For 11 minutes the giddy chase continued. Walker himself wrote:

> I was surprised to find later by the plot that *Stork* had turned three complete circles. . . . I kept the U-boat illuminated with 'Snowflakes' which were quite invaluable in this unusual action. Some rounds of 4-inch were fired from the forward mountings until the guns could not be sufficiently depressed, after which the guns' crews were reduced to shaking fists and roaring curses at an enemy who several times seemed to be a matter of a few feet away rather than yards. . . .
>
> Eventually at 0448 I managed to ram her just before the conning tower from an angle of about 20 degrees on her starboard quarter and roll her over.

She hung for a few seconds on the bow and again on the asdic dome and then scraped aft where she was greeted by a ten-charge pattern at shallowest settings.

Stork and the corvette *Samphire* picked up survivors from *Stanley* and from the U-boat, 28 British and 18 Germans, before shaping course to rejoin the convoy. On the way they came across the hulk of the *Ruckinge*, with the master, chief officer and 12 of her crew in a boat lying off. They were taken aboard *Stork*; *Samphire* was left to deal with *Ruckinge*—eventually to sink her as there could be no hope of salving her. The remainder of *Ruckinge*'s crew had been rescued by the S.S. *Finland* whose master had gallantly dropped back to do so, ignoring the risk involved. In the darkness the master's boat had not been found.

With daylight Walker was able to survey the results of the night's operations. Only one ship of the convoy, the *Ruckinge*, had been hit and a third U-boat destroyed had been added to the score, at the cost of a bent bow to the *Stork* and her asdic put out of action. The loss of *Stanley*, with her Commanding Officer and so many of her crew, was a harsh price to pay, nevertheless, and the battle was by no means over, as the familiar sight of two Kondors on the horizon told. The blue weather had now gone. Two fighters from *Audacity* managed to intercept the Kondors as they dodged in and out of the clouds, shooting down one and damaging the other. In the afternoon another put in an appearance and was also shot down. Then one of *Audacity*'s aircraft reported a submarine seven miles on the port beam of the convoy. Three escorts sped away and, though they made no contact, the U-boat was put down and discouraged from attempting any attack that night.

It was evident, however, that the heavy blows inflicted on the enemy had not brought the enemy's effort to an end. At U-boat headquarters there had been concern and even dismay as evidence of mounting losses came in. Besides the three boats sunk by the escort of HG76, another had been destroyed on the 15th December by the Australian destroyer *Nestor* on patrol off Cape St. Vincent. Dönitz had been faced with the alternatives of calling off the survivors of his pack, reduced now to three, or sending reinforcements to them. Ignorant as yet of the unusual strength of the escort, he chose the latter. Three U-boats, commanded by experienced captains were ordered to the scene—*U71*, *U751* (Korvetten-Kapitän Bigalk) and *U567*, whose captain was the reigning 'ace' of the U-boat fleet, Korvetten-Kapitän Endrass.

While waiting for these reinforcements, the other U-boats hovered on the horizon but forebore to attack. Walker's last fast escorts, *Blankney* and *Exmoor*, had left on the 18th, so that reports from *Audacity*'s aircraft of submarines and sight of them from the *Stork*'s crow's nest could be met only by sending out his slow corvettes to keep them at a distance. By the afternoon of the 21st December 'the net of U-boats seemed to be growing uncomfortably close in spite of *Audacity*'s heroic efforts to keep them at arm's length', Walker noted. He decided to try a ruse to shake them off. As soon as darkness fell the convoy was to alter sharply to a new course, while four of his escorts, pushed out in another direction, would stage a mock battle, firing starshell and 'Snowflakes' to draw the enemy away on a false scent. These moves were duly carried out but his plan was ruined through over-eager masters in the convoy who, ignorant of what was afoot, joined in the pyrotechnic display by firing their 'Snowflakes'. It was doubly unfortunate in that, for the sake of the plan, Walker had reduced the escorts round the convoy and the 'Snowflakes' in the convoy made it a perfect aiming mark. A few minutes later the S.S. *Annavore*, rear ship of the centre column, was torpedoed. This was the only casualty from amongst the merchant ships. But even while the escorts were performing their 'Buttercup' operation, a success which bid fair to even the scores in this long-drawn battle fell to the U-boats.

At dusk *Audacity*, in accordance with Mackendrick's usual custom, had moved out from the vicinity of the convoy. Before leaving, Mackendrick had asked if a corvette could be spared to accompany him, but Walker had been forced to refuse as only four escorts were at that time in close company with the convoy. Learning that Mackendrick was intending to manœuvre to the starboard side of the convoy, Walker had suggested that the port side would be preferable, as it was from the starboard side that the U-boats were expected to approach. However, Mackendrick thought that the convoy's intended alteration of course to port soon after dark would inconvenience him, and eventually *Audacity* went off alone to star-board. Thus it was that, as *U751* was cautiously approaching on the surface, the illuminations and confusing criss-cross movements of escorts showing that the thoroughly alarmed convoy was an un-healthy place for him to be, Korvetten-Kapitän Bigalk suddenly found a long, dark shape silhouetted against the distant lights. He thought at first it was a tanker, but then realised it was a carrier—a heaven-sent target for any U-boat commander. Out of a salvo of torpedoes, one hit *Audacity* on the port side of her engine room, flooding it and bringing the ship to a standstill. Bigalk now boldly approached to point blank range to put two more torpedoes into her. Within ten minutes *Audacity* had gone. Satisfied with this success, Bigalk turned away and made no further attempt to get at the convoy.

There, indeed, a highly confused situation existed. The messages coming over the radio-telephone to Walker reported widely scattered activity by his escorts. Operation 'Buttercup' had brought no con-tact to the *Stork*. Having no asdic since her ramming of *U574*, this could only have been from a sighting in any case. The operation completed, *Stork* resumed her station ahead of the convoy. In the meantime Walker had ordered the *Marigold* and *Convolvulus* to go to the aid of *Audacity*. *Marigold*, however, had not at first been able to comply as she was busy hunting a U-boat which she had sighted on the port side of the convoy. Then came a signal from *Samphire* that she was in asdic contact on the starboard side and was attacking, which she continued to do for some two hours. An hour later *Deptford*, on the other side, sighted a submarine evidently trying to get through to the convoy. Illuminating with starshell, at which the U-boat dived, *Deptford*, too, stuck doggedly to her asdic contact, delivering attack after attack until the contact was finally lost. Somewhere amongst the almost continuous thud and rumble of depth-charges, *U567*, the boat of Korvetten-Kapitän Endrass, had met its end. Which of the escorts was responsible is not known, for *U567* was lost without trace.

There was to be one other startling episode before the night was out. In pitch darkness, *Deptford* was rejoining after her long duel with *U567* (or another). Officers and look-outs, weary after four days of unceasing action, failed to see the *Stork*. As Walker reported the incident,

> At 0517 on the 22nd I was aroused by an unusually ominous crash and came up to find *Deptford*'s stem about one-third of the way into the port side of my quarterdeck. The damage was serious enough but not vital since the main engines and the steering gear (by an inch or two) had not been touched. The after cabin flat was wide open to the elements but the wardroom flat and tiller flat were tight.
>
> *Deptford*'s stem had walked straight into the temporary prison (of survivors of *U574*) and two of the five Boches were pulped, literally, into a bloody mess.

Dawn on the 22nd December, the sixth day of this memorable running fight, came at last to the escorts' weary crews. There had been little sleep for any of them since it had begun. They were reaching the end of their tether. Even the indomitable Walker confessed to finding the outlook gloomy. His own ship was badly damaged both fore and aft, reduced to a maximum speed of 10 knots and bereft of most of her offensive capabilities. *Deptford* had her asdic put out of action and was also reduced in speed. *Stanley* had gone with many of her crew. Above all the *Audacity* and her tireless aircraft were no longer throwing their protective umbrella over the convoy. Against this there was the satisfaction of knowing that in face of a concentrated and persistent attack only two ships of the convoy had been torpedoed, while three U-boats were known to have been destroyed. (The number was in fact four but this was not known till later.)

Relief was, in fact, at hand. For that morning there came the welcome sight of a friendly aircraft, one of the four-engined, very-long-range Liberators which had recently, at long last, been released to Coastal Command. It had come 800 miles from its base to provide air escort, a great advance on the capabilities of the aircraft available up to that time: an augury of developments which were eventually to play a leading part in the defeat of the U-boats. On this occasion the Liberator found U-boats still lingering disconsolately in the vicinity of the convoy and attacked them with depth-charges. The time had come for Dönitz to call off his boats from this unexpectedly prickly hedgehog. The operation was finally abandoned.

The battle for HG76 was of importance for several reasons. In spite of painful losses on both sides, each classified it as a notable victory for the convoy escorts. The loss of four U-boats, including that of Dönitz's most experienced and skilful commander, and several Kondor aircraft, was to some extent offset by the loss of Britain's first and at that time only auxiliary aircraft-carrier. But the fact remained that nine U-boats had been unable to deliver more than two hasty, tip-and-run attacks on a convoy with which they had been in touch for a full week. Though the strength of the escort was much in excess of anything which could as yet be provided on the trans-Atlantic routes, HG76 made it plain that the counter to the U-boat—trained escort groups and a combined sea-and-air escort— existed and, as Britain's resources grew, would eventually win. The writing was on the wall.

Dönitz's staff perceived it. In his *Memoirs* he writes, 'After this failure and in view of the unsatisfactory results of the preceding two months, my staff was inclined to voice the opinion that we were no longer in a position successfully to combat the convoy system because of recent experiences.' Dönitz did not agree:

> The weather and the exceptional strength of the escort had combined to create a situation more than usually unfavourable for a submarine attack. This one isolated case was no reason for making any fundamental change in my views with regard to attacks on convoys and I was proved right by subsequent events. Indeed it was to be in 1942 and the first months of 1943 that we were destined to fight our biggest convoy battles. The successes achieved were enormous.

The German Admiral was only justified in his views by the inability of the Allies, during the time he mentions, to profit by the old lessons re-learnt in the fight for HG76. Of these the greatest was the necessity for continuous air cover if the attacks of U-boat packs were to be defeated. Its eventual provision, at the very time that Dönitz was claiming 'enormous' success, was to force him, in May 1943, to concede victory to the Allies in the North Atlantic. Be that as it may, at the end of December 1941, both sides were poised for what might have been the decisive clash in the Atlantic. It would have been a clash which, with Dönitz's strength reduced by the dispersal of his U-boats in other theatres—the Mediterranean and the Arctic—and with Allied forces growing in strength and improved in performance by the addition of centimetric radar, High Frequency Direction Finders and more efficient asdic equipment, might well have gone overwhelmingly in the Allied favour.

It was not to be. On the 7th December, 1941, Japan had treacherously attacked the United States naval base at Pearl Harbour. Four days later Germany joined the Japanese by declaring war on America. A whole new sea area, packed with unprotected shipping of vital importance to the Allies, was thrown open to the U-boats' depredations. There was no cause to pit themselves against convoys, to range the wide Atlantic wastes in search of such dangerous prey, when the fruit of American unpreparedness for war could be had by shaking the tree.

When the British steamer *Cyclops* was sunk on the 12th January, 1942, off the American eastern seaboard, steering independently and unescorted along the regular coastwise route, it was the beginning of a holocaust of shipping such as had never before been seen.

8

Havoc on the American Coasts

THE DECLARATION OF WAR by Germany on the United States of America on the 11th December, 1941, from the German point of view, only regularised a situation which had for some time existed in the North Atlantic. Step by step the American Government had been steadily increasing its aid to Britain and her Allies. As long ago as July 1940 President Roosevelt had announced that his Government's policy was 'all aid [to Britain] short of war'. In the same month had come the agreement in principle to the exchange of leases of British bases in the Western Hemisphere for 50 old U.S. destroyers. March 1941 saw the passage of the Lend-Lease Bill under which 10 U.S. coastguard cutters were transferred to the Royal Navy. The next month the American Defence Zone was extended to 25 degrees west—more than half-way across the Atlantic.

These developments were, plainly enough, in direct aid to Britain and hostile in intent to Germany. It was not, however, until July 1941, when American troops relieved the British garrison in Iceland and the U.S. Navy was ordered to escort convoys to and from Iceland—convoys which merchant ships of any flag might join—that a real danger of warlike incidents between German U-boats and U.S. naval forces came into existence. That the American Government accepted this possibility became clear, when, on the 1st September, 1941, the U.S. Navy began also to take a share in escorting trans-Atlantic convoys in the western half of the ocean on the disingenuous grounds that they included ships for Iceland. The situation could not yet be described as undeclared war. It was more of the nature of an uneasy armed truce in which any trigger-happy person on either side could start active hostilities. Such an incident occurred on the 4th September, 1941.

The U.S. destroyer *Greer,* proceeding independently to Iceland, received a signal from a patrolling British aircraft that a U-boat had been seen to submerge 10 miles ahead of her. The American captain at once increased speed and on a zig-zag course made for the position given him. Reaching it, he slowed down, put his asdic into operation and very soon was in contact with the submarine. This he held, without attacking, for some three hours. When the aircraft again signalled to the *Greer,* asking if she was intending to attack, the reply was 'No'. The aircraft then dropped its load of depth-charges more or less at random and set course for base. The captain of the U-boat understandably attributed these depth-charges to the destroyer. When the opportunity came he fired a torpedo at the *Greer* in retaliation. This the destroyer was able to avoid, after which she in turn counter-attacked with depth-charges. A second torpedo from the U-boat failed to find its mark and, when the *Greer* lost contact soon afterwards, her captain continued his passage to Iceland.

President Roosevelt pronounced the U-boat's act to be piracy. A few days later he announced that 'From now on if German or Italian vessels of war enter these waters they do so at their own peril'. This gave American ships of war the right to strike first in any encounter with U-boats. An undeclared state of war between the U.S.A. and Germany thus existed in the North Atlantic as from that date. The first clashes were not long in coming.

The first trans-Atlantic convoy to be escorted by United States warships was HX150, which sailed from Halifax on the 16th September, 1941. Had the concentration of U-boats off Greenland not been discovered through the devastating attack on SC42 described in an earlier chapter, and HX150 diverted clear of it, this first wholly American escort must have found itself involved thus early in a full-scale convoy battle. In the event it passed on unmolested and it was not until October that the American and German Navies had their next encounter. This occurred when SC48 was beset on the 15th October, 1941. To its aid were sent five U.S. destroyers from Iceland. During a heavy night attack one of them, the *Kearney,* was torpedoed and badly damaged, suffering a number of casualties.

Fourteen days later the U.S.S. *Reuben James*, one of an American escort to HX156, was torpedoed and sunk, her casualties amounting to 115 including all her officers.

Thus it might have seemed as though Germany's declaration of war would not greatly alter the situation already existing in the Atlantic. But in fact, as President Roosevelt had shrewdly understood, American intervention on the trans-Atlantic convoy routes had not been sufficient to force Hitler into a general war with the U.S.A. The shipping thronging the routes along the coast of North America from the Caribbean to New York had been left unmolested. Now the whole vast sea area became a war zone, the ships in it open to attack. In view of the hard-won experience of the British in anti-submarine warfare, the fruits of which had been freely and unstintingly made available to the United States Navy, the events which were to follow during the first few months of 1942 were calamitous and, to a great extent, unnecessary. Though war with Germany had for some time been inevitable and foreseen, no steps whatever had been taken to prepare for the institution of a convoy system on the American east coast, along which ran the densest and most valuable stream of shipping in the world at that date, carrying cargoes of cotton, sugar, oil, iron, steel and bauxite.

When Admiral Dönitz learnt on the 9th December, 1941, of the lifting of the frustrating handicaps under which his U-boats had been working, which forbade operations against American ships or operations in the Pan-American security zone, he at once proposed to the Naval High Command that 12 boats should be sent to American east coast waters. He saw the brilliant opportunity being offered; but his clear vision, which never allowed him to waver in his appreciation that their Atlantic shipping was the Allies' most vulnerable point, was denied to the High Command. In his *Memoirs*, Dönitz records that on the 1st January, 1942, he had all told, 91 operational U-boats.

Of these, 23, the most effective part of the U-boat arm, were in the Mediterranean and three more were under orders from Naval High Command to proceed there; six were stationed west of Gibraltar and four were deployed along the Norwegian coast. Of the remainder, 60 per cent were in dockyard hands undergoing repairs prolonged by shortage of labour.

There were only 22 boats at sea and about half of these were *en route* to or from their operational base areas. Thus at the beginning of 1942, after two and a half years of war, there were never more than 10 or 12 boats actively and simultaneously engaged in our most important task, the war on shipping.

Dönitz's proposal to concentrate the force available to him on the American coast was rejected. The Mediterranean was to remain the primary area. It was therefore with only five boats that the attack on American east coast shipping was initiated. The blow fell nevertheless with devastating effect.

Between the 12th and the end of January, 1942, 46 ships had been sunk in the North Atlantic. Of these 40, all sailing independently, had been west of 40 degrees west, mostly off the American seaboard. In February the number rose to 65 ships sunk in American waters, out of a total for the North Atlantic of 71. March saw 86 ships lost in the same area. A slight drop in April to 69 rose again in May to 111, in June to 121. Then, in July, came the introduction of a widespread convoy system from the Gulf of Mexico to Canada. The result was a dramatic change to almost total immunity in the areas where previously the sea had been littered with burning and sinking ships. These figures are vividly reminiscent of those in 1917 when a similar holocaust, which had brought Britain to the brink of total defeat, was stopped at once by the introduction of convoy. It is sad to relate that, in spite of this example before them and of further lessons passed on to them from experience in the Second World War, the American naval authorities still held to doctrines and methods whose falsity had been starkly exposed.

The ultimate responsibility for the defence of shipping in American waters belonged to the Commander-in-Chief of the U.S. Atlantic Fleet, Admiral Ernest J. King. Soon after the outbreak of war, King was elevated to the post of Commander-in-Chief, U.S. Fleet, while that of Commander-in-Chief, Atlantic Fleet, fell to Admiral R. E. Ingersoll. King remained the guiding genius of American naval strategy, however, and it was his views which decided the broad lines on which naval forces were employed.

In addition to the ships and aircraft of the Atlantic Fleet, there were other forces under the operational control of the local naval

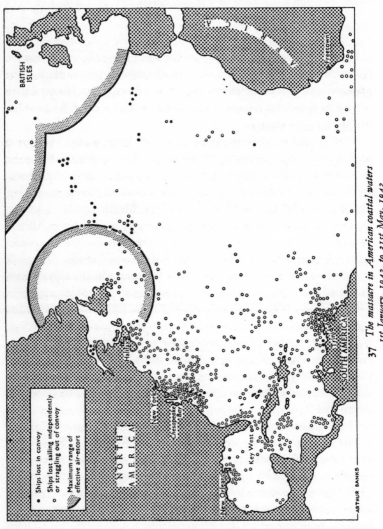

ARTHUR BANKS

37 *The massacre in American coastal waters*
1st January, 1942, to 31st May, 1942

- Ships lost in convoy
- Ships lost sailing independently or straggling out of convoy
- Maximum range of effective air-escort

NORTH AMERICA

BRITISH ISLES

SOUTH AMERICA

New York

Halifax

Chesapeake Bay

Key West

NEW ORLEANS

FREETOWN

commands known as Sea Frontiers. These were certainly inadequate in numbers and quality for the task which faced them. So
far as surface craft were concerned they consisted of coastguard
cutters, converted yachts and a few armed trawlers lent by the
British. Specialised anti-submarine craft were being built, but, owing
to a mistaken conception of the type of ship required, they were
fast, light craft to hunt U-boats instead of more sea-worthy, if less
glamorous, craft for escort duties. The submarine-chasers, as they
were called, proved unsuitable for anti-submarine work in anything
but the calmest weather.

With regard to aircraft the situation was even worse. An Army
Appropriation Act passed by Congress in 1920 had decreed that the
U.S. Army should control all land-based planes and the Navy sea-
based aircraft. In consequence the U.S. Army absorbed almost the
entire supply of U.S. military, land-based planes. It had not even
a component equivalent to Coastal Command of the R.A.F. which,
however inadequately, was trained to fly over the sea and co-operate
with the Royal Navy. U.S. Army pilots were neither trained in
shipping protection duties nor to bomb small moving targets such
as submarines. Nevertheless, at the outbreak of war it was upon
aircraft of the U.S. Army that the U.S. Navy had to rely for anti-
submarine patrols and searches. The inexperience and lack of training of the pilots no doubt made the shortage of aircraft of less
consequence; but, in fact, in January 1942 the air effort in the area of
the Eastern Sea Frontier, covering some 600 miles of the Atlantic
coast, consisted of two daylight sweeps every 24 hours by six short-
range Army bombers. This paucity of anti-submarine forces available
to the Commander Eastern Sea Frontier, Admiral Adolphus
Andrews, was made the argument to show that the institution of a
convoy system was impossible. American naval thought had gained
less than might have been expected from the experiences of the
British in two world wars. The same belief in the purely defensive
—and therefore discreditable—nature of convoy, the same pursuit
of the offensive against an infinitely elusive enemy, had to be paid
for in millions of tons of shipping and vital cargoes.

It was not any mistrust of convoy as the basic means of protecting
shipping which befogged U.S. naval thought. Indeed, in the face of

their own experience in the protection of trans-Atlantic shipping this could hardly be so. Furthermore they must have had in mind the dictum of their own great seaman of the First World War, Admiral W. S. Sims, who had written at that time:

> Our tactics should be such as to force the submarine to incur this danger [that of encountering the escorts] in order to get within range of merchantmen. It, therefore, seems to go without question that the only course for us to pursue is to revert to the ancient practice of convoy. This will be purely an offensive action because, if we concentrate our shipping into convoy and protect it with our naval forces, we will thereby force the enemy, in order to carry out his mission, to encounter naval forces . . . we will have adopted the essential principle of concentration while the enemy will lose it.

In spite of this admirable and irrefutable argument, two fatal objections to its acceptance were raised by the U.S. naval authorities concerned. The official American naval historian, Professor Morison, says that the Commander Eastern Sea Frontier 'knew that a convoy without adequate protection is worse than none'. His forces were therefore employed on 'patrolling the sea lanes' and hunting for U-boats when they betrayed their positions by sinking merchantmen. They were invariably unsuccessful. Not one U-boat was sunk off the American coast until April. Meanwhile so totally unprotected were the merchant ships steaming independently within sight of the shore that U-boats were able to pick them off, one by one, and even to surface and sink them by gunfire. Had only the meagre forces available to Admiral Andrews been used to escort convoys, however 'inadequately', experience elsewhere shows that a U-boat would have been unlikely to sink more than one or two ships, probably at the expense of most of her torpedoes. The Admiral's contention that a 'convoy without adequate protection is worse than none' cannot therefore be accepted.

The other objection to the institution of convoy stemmed from a misreading of the situation. Having studied, and experienced, the pack tactics used against Atlantic convoys in mid-ocean, the Americans evidently assumed that the same methods of protection and similar escort forces would be necessary for coastal convoys; whereas, in fact, pack tactics could never be brought into play close to an enemy coast where reinforcements, air and surface, for a convoy beset could quickly be summoned to the scene. Thus, a Committee, appointed by Admiral King in February 1942 to study the subject, reported:

> It should be borne in mind that effective convoying depends upon the escorts being in sufficient strength to permit their taking the offensive against attacking submarines without their withdrawal for this purpose resulting in unduly exposing the convoy to other submarines while they are on this mission. Any protection less than this simply results in the convoy's becoming a convenient target for submarines.
>
> As a result of experience in the North Atlantic it now appears that the minimum strength that will afford reasonable protection is five escorts per convoy of 40 to 50 ships.

An admirable summary of the situation in mid-Atlantic, but, remembering that the U-boat campaign on the American coast was being conducted by only five U-boats, all operating separately, it was quite out of touch with the situation there. Nevertheless, Admiral King wrote on the 2nd April that 'the principles enunciated and the general procedure suggested in this excellent report are concurred in'. On the basis of it he decided that until more escorts became available a convoy system would have to wait. It is necessary, therefore, to examine the numbers of anti-submarine ships and aircraft which were actually available. Professor Morison in discussing this question quotes only the figure of those available for the exclusive use of the Sea Frontier Commander—'pitifully inadequate' he calls them, with which we will not disagree. But, in fact, there was also available in the area a considerable force of destroyers of the U.S. Atlantic Fleet. In the face of a violent newspaper agitation for something to be done, Admiral Andrews asked for 15 of them in February. He got seven. These were sent out on patrol which proved uniformly futile. Racing from one spot to another in which U-boats had been located, they never succeeded in gaining contact with any of them. Professor Morison comments:

> No scientific method of search to regain sound contact with a submarine had been worked out. U.S. destroyers were then so ill-fitted for search and so imperfectly trained for attack that to use them as a roving patrol was worse than useless. It resulted only in the loss of the *Jacob Jones* [torpedoed on the 28th February].

While Morison is no doubt justified in his criticism of the efficiency of U.S. destroyers—a shortcoming not unusual in the armed forces of a country freshly involved in war—he is not justified in ascribing the uselessness of roving patrols to this cause. Statistics and the experience of the most skilled anti-submarine forces show that hunting and patrol unrelated to the movement of a convoy—the lure which must draw U-boats to it if they are to fulfil their mission—are rarely effective. The point is, however, that, had there been an appreciation of the prime necessity to get merchant ships into convoy at all costs, escorts could have been found. It will be recalled that convoy was instituted by the British on the outbreak of war with an available escort strength of 112 surface vessels and 45 aircraft. Opposed to them were 18 U-boats—a number which rarely dropped below 14 for the remainder of 1939. According to the U.S. Fleet Anti-Submarine Summary produced in July 1945, the anti-submarine forces available to the Americans in the North Atlantic in January 1942 comprised 173 surface craft and 268 aircraft. In April the number of surface craft was the same but aircraft had risen to 589. In the middle of May, when shipping losses were reaching intolerable proportions, convoy was at last instituted on the United States east coast, the average size of convoy being about 21 ships and of escorts never less than five. The publication quoted above gives the figures of anti-submarine forces available as 197 surface vessels and 643 aircraft.

Thus, if Admiral King's contention that convoy could not be instituted in January 1942 on account of shortage of escorts is to be accepted, it appears that the addition of 24 escort vessels was sufficient completely to reverse the situation and put ships into convoy with a comparatively lavish escort. The improbability of this makes it seem more likely that a change of heart took place in American naval circles as a result of the complete failure of their 'offensive' methods. This is borne out by an exchange of messages between Admiral King and General Marshall, Chief of Staff of the United States Army. The latter was deeply concerned at the heavy losses of army transports:

> We are well aware of the limited number of escort craft available, but has every conceivable means been brought to bear on this situation?

I am fearful that another month or two of this will so cripple our means of transport that we will be unable to bring sufficient men and planes to bear against the enemy in critical theatres to exercise a determining influence on the war.

In his reply, King announced his views with all the fervour of a convert. 'Escort is not just one way of handling the submarine menace; it is the *only* way that gives any promise of success. The so-called patrol and hunting operations have time and again proved futile.' How different from the reply given to Admiral Pound, First Lord of the Admiralty, when he told King on the 19th March, 1942, that he 'regarded the introduction of convoy as a matter of urgency'. Like Admiral Andrews, King at that time pronounced that 'inadequately escorted convoys were worse than none'.

Enough has been said, however, to establish the fact that it was primarily the complete organisational unpreparedness of the Americans, coupled with a failure to benefit from the lessons so hardly learnt by their Allies, that provided the U-boat commanders with the second of their 'Happy Times' and exposed American and Allied shipping to an unprecedented massacre. It remains to record the magnitude of the disaster and the means whereby it was encompassed.

Dönitz's first five boats—long-endurance, 1,000-ton boats—set out from their Biscay base at the end of December 1941, 'taking with them', the Admiral writes, 'high hopes such as we at U-boat Command had not had for many a day'. These hopes were to be richly fulfilled. Though America had had five weeks grace in which to prepare for the assault, the U-boats found conditions little different from those of peace. Ships steamed independently along the normal routes, their navigation lights burning. Lighthouses, beacons and buoys flashed their signals though with reduced brilliancy. As for defensive measures, Dönitz records:

> There were, admittedly, anti-submarine patrols, but they were wholly lacking in experience. Single destroyers, for example, sailed up and down the traffic lanes with such regularity that the U-boats were quickly able to work out the time-table being followed. They knew exactly when the destroyers would return, and the knowledge only added to their sense of security during the intervening period.

In such conditions the U-boats could attack at leisure and in complete safety. By day they lay on the bottom in security, surfacing at dusk to pick their targets from the defenceless stream of shipping. This was made all the easier by the brilliant illuminations of the coast resorts against which the ships stood out in clear silhouette.

These first five boats, working between the St. Lawrence and Cape Hatteras, not unnaturally had a great and easy success. Three more large boats joined them off Chesapeake Bay before the end of January and added to the havoc being caused. Between them they sank no less than 40 ships between the 13th January and the end of the month. Their achievements led Dönitz to decide to deploy his whole available strength in the western Atlantic. New boats completing their training in the Baltic were ordered as soon as ready to make for the Biscay bases at high speed, there to be prepared to cross to America. But at this moment Hitler's 'intuition' came to the Allies' aid.

Believing that an Allied invasion of Norway was planned, he gave orders for eight boats to be stationed in the north for its protection. Once again Dönitz found himself frustrated at the moment that a resounding triumph seemed imminent. He decided, therefore, that his smaller, 750-ton boats, which up to now had been operating off Nova Scotia and Newfoundland, must be used to reinforce the attack on the American shipping. In the north these smaller boats had found little but driving snow, ice and winter gales. The first group, having arrived on their station after some of their fuel had already been expended on patrol off the Azores, could not be diverted to the new happy hunting ground. The next group of 750-tonners, however, were sent to operate south of Halifax. Owing to their limited endurance, it had not been expected that they would be able to remain long on station. But enthusiasm to take full advantage of the conditions off the American coast led their engineers to try a number of ingenious methods of saving fuel on passage. In addition, water tanks were used for fuel, while the crews' living quarters were cluttered with stores, spare parts and food so that they might remain longer in so fruitful an area. Thus they were able to press on southwards to New York and beyond, and remain there for two or three weeks.

In the meantime a second wave of five 1,000-ton boats had already crossed the Atlantic bound for the Caribbean. By the 16th February they were on station, and Dönitz gave the order for a simultaneous attack. Now the whole length of the American coast from Trinidad to New York became the graveyard of Allied shipping. Wolfgang Frank, author of *The Sea Wolves*, describes the happy conditions that the U-boat commanders found.

> There was still no evidence that the Americans were switching over to war-time conditions. After two months of war their ships were still sailing independently. Their captains stopped close to torpedoed ships and asked for information over the loud hailer: should a ship be hit but remain capable of steaming, the captain never bothered to zig-zag or vary his speed so as to impede the U-boat in dealing the coup-de-grace. And they had no idea of security; they chattered about everything under the sun over the 600-metre wave band—and as if that were not enough, the coastal defence stations sent out over the air a regula, programme of information, giving details of rescue work in progressr of where and when aircraft would be patrolling and the schedules of anti-submarine vessels.

Gradually, however, these aids to the U-boats were reduced. In the four months following the opening of the U-boat offensive, the Americans tried everything—except convoy—to master the situation. Ships were routed close in shore, which only served to increase the density of the traffic stream and worried the U-boats not at all. Then shipping was restricted to moving only in daylight anchoring for the night in Chesapeake or Delaware Bays or in protected anchorages prepared for them. By this system, known as the 'Bucket Brigade', Jacksonville to New York could be made in four daylight runs. In spite of all, the shipping losses mounted steeply. The U-boat commanders brought a light-hearted verve to their work of destruction in conditions so much less rigorous than the pursuit of escorted convoys in the gales and fogs of the north. Wolfgang Frank records how one of them, Jochen Mohr of *U124*, reporting a score of nine ships sunk during his patrol did so in verse,

> *The new-moon night is black as ink*
> *Off Hatteras the tankers sink*
> *While sadly Roosevelt counts the score*
> *Some fifty thousands—by Mohr.*

But at last, in May, the Americans were ready to institute a convoy system along their coast. The result is best given in Dönitz's own words:

> At the end of April the heavy sinkings off the east coast of America suddenly ceased. As this was a full moon period, I hoped that the dark nights to follow would restore the situation and that the sinkings would regain their previous high level. Instead, there was a steady increase in signals from the U-boats reporting no shipping sighted. . . .
>
> In the light of unfavourable conditions off the east coast of America and favourable conditions in the Caribbean, U-boat Command at once transferred six boats from the former area to the latter and four further U-boats on the way to American waters from the Biscay ports were sent to the Caribbean.

Thus the simple act of gathering the merchant shipping together in groups, and removing the stream of independently sailing ships, achieved what had been previously considered impossible unless escorts in sufficient numbers to take the offensive could be provided. It was a remarkable vindication of the convoy system. So long, however, as the system was not extended to the Gulf of Mexico and the Caribbean, Dönitz's assault on Allied shipping could be maintained at the same high level as before. Indeed in May the number of ships sunk was greater than ever before. Forty-one ships of nearly a quarter of a million tons, more than half of which were tankers, were sunk in the Gulf of Mexico alone. Another 38, more than 200,000 tons were sent to the bottom in the Caribbean area.

Up to now sinkings had been limited by the short time the submarines could remain on station after the long passage from France, before they had again to leave with enough fuel and stores remaining for the return journey. On the 21st April there sailed the first of the U-tankers or Milch-cows, *U459*. A large clumsy boat of nearly 1,700 tons, she had no offensive capabilities; but besides a quantity of stores and spare parts she carried 700 tons of diesel fuel of which some 600 tons were available to refuel other boats. In this way she replenished 12 of the smaller and two large U-boats. As a result the number of boats on station in May was greatly increased, about 12 being spread along the American East Coast, nearly 20 in the Gulf of Mexico and Caribbean area. The latter group, roving happily amongst the streams of shipping sailing independently along the established routes from the oil ports and the West Indies, accounted for 148 ships with a total tonnage of 752,009 tons during May and June. In his *Memoirs*, Admiral Dönitz recounts how, in 1957,

> Admiral Hoover, who in 1942 had been in command of the Caribbean and had done everything possible with the naval and air forces at his disposal to stem the onslaught of our boats, wrote me a friendly letter in which he said, 'The years 1945–6 must have been a great strain on your nerves, but 1942, when you conducted your astonishing U-boat war against me in the Caribbean was, for me, an equally nerve-shattering period.'

The strange thing about this extract is that the American Admiral should still, long afterwards, call the operations of Dönitz's U-boats in the area of his Command 'astonishing'; whereas it was in reality his failure to use his forces as convoy escorts, however meagre, that was astonishing. 'From the end of June, however', Dönitz goes on,

> Results in these areas, too, began to deteriorate. Here, too, as had happened off the east coast of the United States at the beginning of May, the convoy system was gradually introduced; and it became obvious that in the near future the main effort of the U-boat war would have to be switched back to wolf-pack attacks on convoys.

So the second 'Happy Time' came to an end. The decisive clash between the wolf-packs and convoy escorts could not much longer be postponed. As in one area after another the Allies closed their ranks and put shipping into escorted convoys, it was to mid-Atlantic, the last region not yet within range of shore-based aircraft, that the U-boats gravitated. There, in the 10 months from July 1942 to May 1943, the battle was to be fought out to a decisive conclusion.

9

The Battle Swings to Mid-Atlantic

ALTHOUGH BY JULY 1942 the period of easy success for his U-boats had been brought to an end by the wide-spread introduction of convoy in American waters, Admiral Dönitz was by no means discouraged, though in a radio speech to the German people he warned them that they must expect greater casualties. The convoys and their escorts would now have to be faced. The decisive struggle was impending. It would be undertaken, he believed, under greatly improved conditions for the Germans. The number of boats available had increased and they should now be better able to intercept the convoys and concentrate against them in the 'black gap' in mid-Atlantic where no air escort could reach.

On the other hand, though Dönitz could not know it, the opposition his boats would be meeting was by now much improved in quality. Most of the escorts had received the new 10-centimetre radar equipment which gave detections of surfaced submarines at ranges of four miles or more. Many of them also had the High Frequency Direction Finder by means of which the bearing and, to some extent, the range of a unit transmitting on short-wave radio could be determined (*see* Appendix). The combination of these two devices made the U-boat tactics of the wolf-pack and the night surface attack far more hazardous than previously. The wireless messages, necessary to keep the U-boat Command informed of the situation and to enable the pack concentration to be effected, gave the escort commander warning of an impending attack. Under favourable circumstances they could betray, with considerable accuracy, the position of the boat which had transmitted, bringing down on it a hunting group detached from the escort. By night, or in thick weather, an approaching submarine could be detected by radar far outside visibility range. Thus, the escorts now had the advantage of the first 'sighting', which the U-boats had enjoyed in those earlier times, when they could approach on the surface, confident that they could see before being seen. The use of radar by night or in fog also meant that the escort commanders were no longer preoccupied with maintaining proper station and avoiding collisions. They could now concentrate exclusively on detection of their lurking enemy.

Once detected, the U-boats also faced a more formidable attack. No longer could they gain immunity by diving to great depths. Depth-charges were now available which could be set to explode at a depth of 500 feet. Furthermore, escorts were fitted to fire patterns of 10 charges, giving a greater probability of one of the charges exploding at a lethal distance from the target. Should the enemy remain at lesser depths and hope to evade attack by agility of manœuvre, another weapon was now beginning to be fitted in the escorts. Known as the 'Hedgehog', this was a multi-barrelled mortar which fired bombs, filled with a new, higher-powered explosive, Torpex, to a fixed range of 250 yards ahead of the ship. This form of attack, unlike a depth-charge attack, gave the submarine no warning to enable it to take evasive action (*see* Appendix).

The problem of maintaining escorts at full strength for the whole of the long trans-Atlantic voyage had been eased by the introduction of a system of re-fuelling at sea from tankers sailed with the convoys for this purpose. The operation required reasonably good weather, however. Another innovation at this time, though actually a lesson from the First World War re-learnt, was the inclusion in convoys of specially fitted rescue ships. Their duty was to pick up survivors from sunken ships. They thus relieved the escort commander of the necessity to divert one or more of his few ships at the expense of hunting down the attackers. By now, also, many of the escort group commanders and the captains of the individual escort ships, after many months engaged in the specialised business of convoy escort, had achieved an 'expertise' which only time could give them. They had developed an instinct which enabled them to weed out false alarms and to know when it was possible and politic to thin out the defensive screen so as to go over to the attack. They were able to see into their opponents' minds and foresee their probable tactics. Thus it was not only the improved methods of detection which led to U-boat commanders suffering the frustration of being discovered and driven off, time after time.

For all these improvements, however, the escorts were still weak numerically. The U.S. Navy's heavy commitments elsewhere, in the Pacific as well as along their Atlantic coast and in escorting troop and transport convoys to the Mediterranean, had led to its virtual withdrawal from the North Atlantic. This left the Royal Navy to shoulder 50 per cent of the burden in that vital area and the Royal Canadian Navy 46 per cent. America's four per cent was represented by one or two coastguard cutters which led a mixed escort of American, British and Canadian ships, and a few destroyers based in Iceland. Early in 1943 the latter were also withdrawn, but their departure was more than compensated for by the formation of the U.S. escort carrier *Bogue* and her destroyer screen into a Support Group in March of that year. Though British and Canadian forces had grown considerably since the early days of the struggle, at this time they still averaged only five or six escorts to each convoy, a figure much below the minimum required. Not all of them had yet received the new equipment. Nor had they all achieved the same standard of training, either individually or as flotillas. Thus much would still depend upon the relative efficiency of the opponents when they met in combat around the convoys.

Such was the general situation in the summer of 1942 when the contest in mid-Atlantic was resumed in August. It followed the course predictable from a full knowledge of the factors which prevailed on both sides. A majority of the convoys ran without loss; either because, through skilful diversion by order of the shore command, based on the information collected by the U-boat tracking organisation, the submarine patrol lines were avoided; or because air or surface escorts were able to detect and hold down, drive off or perhaps destroy the first U-boat making contact, thereby preventing the position and route of the convoy being reported.

But where the escort was weak, ill-assorted or lacking in group training, the wolves were able to gather round. Such was the case with the slow, homeward-bound convoy of 36 ships, SC94, which was beset in the first week of August 1942. The ocean escort was not unduly weak numerically, comprising as it did six small warships. But of these only one was a destroyer, H.M.C.S. *Assiniboine*, commanded by Lieutenant-Commander J. H. Stubbs, R.C.N. The remainder, including the ship of the senior officer of the escort, H.M.S. *Primrose*, were corvettes. Such ships, besides being too slow to chase away any U-boats working round the convoy to their attacking positions ahead, were unable to mount the H/F D/F equipment; nor had they, for the most part, the new 10-centimetre radar. When the *Assiniboine* was damaged and forced to return to base, the odds turned heavily in favour of the U-boats. Individually, the escorts were well-trained and experienced. On the other hand, they had not been trained to work together; nor was a Flower-class corvette a suitable ship, on account of space or equipment, from which to exercise command. It was by the accident of seniority of rank, that Lieutenant-Commander A. Ayre, R.N.R., of the *Primrose*, found himself called upon to do so.

In the five days' running fight which began on the afternoon of the 5th August, these disadvantages were to prove calamitous. During the 3rd, SC94 had been enveloped in the dense fog which hangs over the Grand Banks at this time of the year. When an alteration of course was ordered by the Commodore by signal on the siren, six ships on the port side failed to hear and, with the two escorts on that side, *Nasturtium* and *Orillia*, became detached from the main body. It was not until the afternoon of the 5th August, by which time the weather had cleared somewhat, that the senior officer of the escort learnt their whereabouts and sent *Assiniboine* out to contact and shepherd them back into the fold. Before this could be effected the first blow fell as one of the stragglers, the S.S. *Spar*, was torpedoed and sunk.

No contact with the attacker was made. The first round had gone to the enemy. What was worse, the U-boat was left free to follow, to see the junction with the main body and report the convoy's position and course. Soon the other boats of the patrol line were running hard on the surface to intercept. Towards midday on the 6th the first arrived. Fog patches, lingering over the calm sea, hid the convoy until, as the U-boat ran out of one, it was suddenly in

sight at six miles. At the same moment the U-boat was seen from
the bridge of the *Assiniboine*. Followed by the corvette *Dianthus*, the
destroyer swung away in chase, forcing the submarine to seek safety
by diving. *Assiniboine*'s asdic went into operation and as contact was
gained the depth-charges were sent plunging down. Three attacks
were made before contact was lost. With *Dianthus* in company,
Assiniboine searched, probing with the asdic, weaving in and out of
the fog patches. It seemed as though her quarry had given her the
slip.

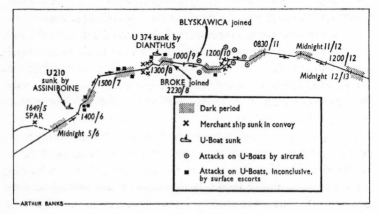

38   *The passage of convoy SC94, August 1942*

But the depth-charges had done their work. Heavy damage had
accumulated in the U-boat. She was forced to come up and try to
escape on the surface. Sighted by the *Assiniboine* at five miles range,
a wild chase through the fog patches developed. As the destroyer
overhauled the submarine, gun crews on both sides went into
action. A shell hit the submarine's conning-tower. In reply a shot
went home on the starboard side of the destroyer, starting a dangerous fire, killing one man and wounding 13 others. Meanwhile the
U-boat was frantically twisting and turning to avoid Stubbs' efforts
to ram her. Three or four times *Assiniboine*'s sharp bow just failed to
hit her. The destroyer was so close that her guns could not be
depressed sufficiently to be aimed at the submarine almost alongside.
Suddenly the U-boat slowed down. It started to dive. But before it

could do so the *Assiniboine* had clawed round under full helm and rammed. It was not a fatal blow and, as the submarine came fully to the surface, *Assiniboine* again thrust her bow against it in a glancing blow. Sliding on beyond the now stationary boat, the destroyer's depth-charges, set to burst shallow, took up the fight. Then a 4·7-inch shell hit the submarine in the bow and all was over. *U210* went to the bottom as the *Dianthus* slid out of the fog just in time to see her go. Pounding along behind at her best speed trying to get into the fight, the little corvette had only succeeded in being in at the death. But now she had the satisfaction of taking 22 of the enemy prisoners, the remainder being picked up by the *Assiniboine*.

This was a heartening success for the convoy defence. Had it only occurred a day earlier and so disposed of the first submarine to gain contact, that which had torpedoed the *Spar*, the convoy might well have passed through the U-boat patrol line without further trouble. Instead opportunity had been given for the pack to gather. Even while *U210* and *Assiniboine* were playing their deadly game of hide-and-seek amongst the mists, the conning-tower of another submarine had been sighted from the corvettes *Primrose* and *Chilliwack*, ahead of the convoy. Three hours later the corvette *Orillia* was hunting another which she had seen on the surface and forced to dive. Finally, as darkness was settling down a signal came in to the escort commander from *Dianthus* telling him that she, too, on her way back to rejoin, had discovered and was hunting a third. For the time being the situation was in hand. Surprised on the surface through the lifting or parting of the fog, the would-be attackers were being driven off. Three of them were damaged. They were not put out of action, however, and there were several long days ahead in which to renew their efforts. Meanwhile the escort had been reduced to four slow corvettes until the *Dianthus* could rejoin, as the only destroyer, *Assiniboine*, was limping back to base licking the wounds she had received in her action with *U210*.

Nevertheless when, after a quiet day on the 7th, the U-boats renewed their attempts to get at the convoy under cover of darkness they were detected by radar and again held off. With their slow speed, the corvettes could not, however, go over to the offensive with prolonged hunts which would have at least forced their opponents out of the action. Nor could they afford to extend their search beyond the horizon when daylight came. Thus, they could not prevent others of the wolf-pack from using their high surface speed to circle wide round the convoy, attain a position ahead and there wait, submerged, for the convoy to approach. The 8th August was a calm, summer day with only a slight haze to reduce visibility. Through the forenoon and past midday the 32 slow merchantmen plodded eastwards at $7\frac{1}{2}$ knots, while the escorts weaved to and fro in their stations, trying to cover the broad sea miles between them and the neighbouring corvette.

In merchantman and escort alike, watchkeepers who had spent much of the night peering into the darkness, and gun and depthcharge crews who had been in action were taking advantage of the unwonted peace of the hot afternoon to get some sleep against the probability of another night of activity. This placid scene was shattered by a succession of explosions coming across the still air and thudding through the ships' hulls. Within three minutes five merchantmen had been torpedoed. Three of them, including the Commodore's flagship, *Trehata,* went quickly to the bottom. The other two remained afloat for a time. The sudden onset and the extent of the catastrophe sent a wave of panic through the convoy. Three ships stopped engines and their crews took to the boats, while the British gun crew of a Dutch ship leapt overboard. For a time complete confusion reigned. The escorts, instead of being free to hunt the attackers, were forced to devote themselves to picking up survivors from the sunken ships and cajoling the crews of others to return aboard and get their ships under way. The coloured crew of one of the latter, the *Radchurch,* refused to do so and the ship had to be abandoned. Not until shortly before nightfall did the convoy reform itself.

In the meanwhile events had been taking place which were to some extent to even the score temporarily. From the *Dianthus* a conningtower had been sighted on the horizon. At the order of the senior officer of the escort, her captain, Lieutenant-Commander C. E. Bridgeman, R.N.R., took her away in chase. It seemed a forlorn hope as a U-boat on the surface could outpace the corvette. Furthermore, the distant enemy was soon lost in a rain squall. Nevertheless

Bridgeman plugged doggedly on and was rewarded after a time by the sight of not one but two submarines. At a range of six miles, *Dianthus* opened fire with her solitary 4-inch gun. The chances of hitting the tiny targets at that range were remote, but as Bridgeman had hoped, the U-boat commanders, rather than accept the risk, submerged. Half an hour later the corvette had reached the diving position of one of them and had begun a systematic search round it. For an hour and a half this was continued without result. Meanwhile darkness had fallen. Bridgeman had almost decided that he must abandon the hunt and return to the convoy when there came a shout from his signalman. He had a dark object held in his binoculars. It was almost certainly a U-boat. Star shells from *Dianthus'* gun blossoming above it confirmed it. The U-boat dived and almost at once was caught in the asdic beam. Two accurate depth-charge attacks, and *U379* came spouting to the surface heavily damaged. Bridgeman spun his ship round. As *Dianthus* rammed and slid on beyond, further depth-charges were exploded round the crippled submarine. Four more times the corvette crashed into it before, soon after midnight, *U379* sank leaving survivors of its crew in the water. By now *Dianthus* was in a bad way herself with her fore compartments flooded and much down by the bow. Little attention could be given to rescuing the submarine crew; but five of them were taken aboard and a Carley Raft launched for the remainder before Bridgeman set course to rejoin the convoy while his crew turned to to repair the damage to their ship.

While *Dianthus* was away, occupied with her private battle, the convoy had received a welcome reinforcement from Iceland in the shape of the destroyer *Broke,* whose captain, Lieutenant-Commander A. F. C. Layard, became the senior officer of the escort. The situation he found as night fell was not a happy one. The *Primrose* was the only other warship in company, while several U-boats were known to be about and no doubt planning further attacks. The night, however, passed uneventfully. By dawn the convoy had reformed and more corvettes were back in their stations. The Polish destroyer *Blyskawica* was also about to join up. At midday there came the heartening sight of the first of the Liberator aircraft which were thereafter intermittently to accompany and escort the convoy. In conjunction with the H/F D/F now available in the *Broke,* there seemed a good prospect of interrupting the free movement of the enemy and preventing him from reaching an attacking position. Towards evening one of his craft was reported by the aircraft nine miles on the port beam of the convoy. The *Blyskawica* streaked away to hunt it, and keep it down. Shortly before dawn another boat was heard signalling close astern. *Primrose* sent to search along the bearing sighted it, opened fire and forced it to dive. A two-hour asdic search was unproductive, but, as the corvette steered to rejoin the now distant convoy, yet another submarine was sighted, chased and forced to dive.

The U-boats were certainly being harassed. But, as was to be found on other occasions, once the pack had gathered it required continuous air escort, backed by fast escorts, to hold all of them off. During the forenoon of the 10th August the convoy was bereft of air escort, the first aircraft arriving at noon, and meanwhile one or more submarines had evidently achieved a position along the convoy's route. Lying submerged and undetected, their opportunity to attack came at 10.22 a.m., when in quick succession four more merchantmen were torpedoed. In spite of all efforts by the escorts, the attacker escaped scot-free to bring the total casualties up to 11 merchantmen at the price of two U-boats. The ordeal of SC94 was at last at an end. Destroyer reinforcements and a more continuous air escort frustrated all further efforts by the enemy. The much depleted convoy sailed on to its destination without further loss.

The lessons to be learnt from SC94 had already been pointed time and again, and were to be repeated in the future. The capacity of the various units making up the escort to hunt U-boats efficiently was not enough. They must also be trained to work together as a team. The force escorting SC94 was a mixed force of British and Canadian ships thrown together for the occasion. Its senior officer had neither the equipment to hold them together and direct their activities, nor had he had the opportunity to train them to work together with a minimum of direction from their leader. Admiral Dönitz, when he received details of this action, concluded that 'the fact that the boats succeeded in pressing home their attacks in spite of the strength of the escort is the deciding factor which justifies the continuation of our war on convoys'. But in fact the total number of escorts with a convoy was less important than the proportion of escorts with a high turn of speed. Destroyers could thus be sent out to a submarine detected near a convoy, could hunt it for an effective period and return to the convoy before other U-boats could take advantage of the gap left in the screen. The Flower-class corvettes, with a maximum speed of 15 knots could not be used offensively, or, if they were sent out to hunt a submarine, they left the escort weakened for long periods. What was likely to happen then was demonstrated, not for the first or last time, in October 1942. Convoy SL125, homeward bound from Freetown, 37 ships carrying, besides full holds of cargo, a large number of servicemen, was sailed with an ocean escort of only four corvettes. When it ran into a concentration of 10 U-boats north-east of Madeira, the escort under Lieutenant-Commander J. M. Rayner, R.N.R., of the *Petunia*, was helpless to prevent the loss of 12 ships with a tragically heavy toll of life; nor was it able in return to inflict any loss on the enemy.

Another factor which befogged Dönitz's appreciation of the facts of the situation in the Atlantic was that the escort groups varied in the quality of the equipment they carried. At this time the rapidly expanding Royal Canadian Navy, eager to stand on its own feet, had formed its own escort groups which took their turn with the British groups to shepherd convoys on the trans-Atlantic run. In retrospect this must be judged premature, as their ships lagged behind their British sisters in modern equipment, lacking in particular the 10-centimetre radar which was so crucial a device. When a westbound convoy, ON127, with a strong Canadian escort, was brought to action in September 1942, the destroyer *Ottawa* and seven merchant ships were torpedoed and sunk, and four more of the convoy torpedoed and damaged. The U-boats responsible escaped unscathed. Fortunately by the late summer of 1942 regular escort groups had been formed and assigned to the trans-Atlantic run, each of which usually included two destroyers. A convoy escorted by a well-trained and well-led escort group of this kind had little to fear or, if for some reason the escort was unable to prevent the concentration of a wolf-pack on it, the U-boats were likely to be made to pay heavily for any successes they achieved.

Thus in the same month of that year, the slow, homeward-bound convoy SC104 was intercepted by a submarine pack of 13 in the 'black gap' where no air escort could be given it. The enemy's arrival on the scene was at once detected by the H/F D/F operators as they crouched in their cramped cabinets, listening hour after hour to the German radio traffic. The senior officer of the escort, Commander S. Heathcote, in the destroyer *Fame,* had under him another British destroyer, *Viscount,* and four corvettes, *Potentilla, Eglantine, Montbretia* and *Acanthus* of the Royal Norwegian Navy.

As evidence came in to him of the wolf-pack gathering, his ships were sent out at their best speed into the darkness, along the bearings indicated by the direction finders. The weather, a gale from the south-west raising a steep sea with intermittent snow showers, handicapped them, the wild motion of the ships and the tall waves making both radar and asdic inefficient, while the spray sweeping across their bridges blinded look-outs. No submarines were therefore sighted or detected, but these sorties had the desired effect, forcing the U-boats to dive and preventing them getting at the convoy. Nevertheless, it was not possible to drive off every one of such a strong concentration. While the screen was depleted one submarine was able to infiltrate through it and soon after midnight torpedoed and sank three ships of the convoy. Dawn the next day, 13th October, spread over a still wild and stormy sea, but visibility had improved. Escorts sent out towards enemy radio transmissions caught sight of the submarines responsible, but the heavy weather kept speeds low and enabled the U-boats to dive when still many miles away, making very slim the chances of a successful hunt.

At dusk three of the escorts were still away leaving only *Fame, Montbretia* and *Acanthus* to cover the convoy of 44 ships. During the night four more ships of the convoy were sunk. Meanwhile, however, the escorts were not idle, and only the heavy weather saved the wolf-pack from loss. Lieutenant-Commander John Waterhouse of the *Viscount,* for instance, had been coming up from astern to rejoin the screen after a sortie, and was still seven miles behind, when the first attack occurred. Soon afterwards he sighted two stragglers, one of which was the huge whaling depot ship *Southern Empress,* which had been torpedoed but was still able to proceed at slow speed. As Waterhouse watched, two more torpedoes exploded against the *Southern Empress'* side, finally sinking her. Calculating the probable position from which the submarine had fired, Waterhouse steered for it and was rewarded by the sight of her coming to the surface, unaware, no doubt, that a warship was near by. A wild scrambling encounter followed during which Waterhouse's attempt to ram the submarine and *Viscount'*s gunlayers' efforts to get a shell home in her before she dived again were all foiled by the blinding spray and the black darkness. Once the submarine had submerged she was safe, the wild conditions on the surface making operation of *Viscount'*s asdic almost impossible. The convoy being again under attack, Waterhouse set course to rejoin. The other destroyer of the escort, *Fame,* had a similar encounter a few hours later when, following an attack on an asdic contact, a submarine came to the surface. In the chase which developed down wind and swell, from the destroyer's lurching bridge the submarine was hard to distinguish among the white-crested waves. When the range had come down to 500 yards, the U-boat dived again; but this was not at once realised. The *Fame* careered on for a while before turning and trying, unsuccessfully, to regain asdic contact.

Inconclusive as these encounters were, the narrow escapes must certainly have shaken the U-boat commanders concerned and made them chary of approaching the convoy again. The gale began to take off during the next day, 14th October, and the escorts were able to range farther afield keeping the pack at a distance. With nightfall the U-boats probed inwards trying to get at the convoy. But each time they approached the escorts' radar detected them. Out of the darkness came the white flurry of a bow wave forcing them to crash dive and give up the attempt. The *Acanthus* was the first to have such an encounter. In her station on the port beam of the convoy her radar detected something at a range of five miles. Lieutenant-Commander E. Bruun, Royal Norwegian Navy, set off in chase and narrowly missed ramming the submarine which came in sight at 400 yards. The *Montbretia,* Lieutenant-Commander Halvos Soiland, on the other side of the convoy, was the next. In a brief encounter at short range in the darkness, her 4-inch gun put a shell into the U-boat before she was lost to view. It may well have been this same submarine which *Viscount*'s radar picked up an hour later. Running down the radar contact, when the range came down to 2,000 yards Waterhouse ordered 26 knots and steered for a ram. As the U-boat came in sight her commander simultaneously saw the destroyer's sharp bow bearing down on him. Too late he began to weave back and forth to avoid it. The *Viscount*'s stem crunched into her hull, lifted on a wave and crashed down, pinning the submarine down for some 15 seconds before she dragged clear. Her back broken, *U619* plunged to her end. *Viscount* herself was heavily damaged. Until bulkheads forward had been shored up and the fore end of the ship lightened to bring her bows out of water, she dare not go ahead at more than 7 knots. This was increased to 13 when repairs had been completed but her need for the shelter and facilities of a base were urgent. Waterhouse was instructed to carry on alone. The escort was reduced to five but by now, with the improvement in the weather, the fight had fairly turned in favour of the defence. Before dawn *Fame* and *Potentilla* each encountered and attacked other U-boats trying to penetrate the screen. They did not manage to destroy them, though *Fame* hammered one with three depth-charge attacks and *Potentilla* damaged another with gunfire and depth-charges. With daylight the escorts resumed their repeated outward sweeps to drive off others whose signals had been picked up on the H/F D/F.

In his account of the long five days of unceasing action, Commander Heathcote paid tribute to his gallant Norwegians who 'pounced like terriers' whenever an opportunity arose, in spite of the tempestuous weather in which their little corvettes rolled and lurched in wild exhausting motion, swept by spray and their decks awash. Nevertheless, the wolf-pack continued to cling to the outskirts. When the convoy at last came inside the range of Liberator aircraft from Iceland, the first to arrive with sunrise on the 16th October soon reported that it had sighted a submarine and forced it to dive five miles astern. That at least one U-boat had succeeded in pressing on ahead to lie submerged in ambush was to be discovered when, soon after midday the *Fame*, two miles ahead, gained asdic

contact with it. After his many frustrating and disheartening encounters during the preceding days of heavy weather, Commander
Heathcote was now able to employ his anti-submarine team in good
conditions. His first attack forced the U-boat *U353* to the surface.
His ram, which followed, delivered only a glancing blow, the submarine scraping down *Fame*'s starboard side. By now the convoy
had come up. The gunners of the merchantmen passing by to either
side went gaily into action at this first sight of the enemy who had
been tormenting them. It was too much for the U-boat's crew who
abandoned ship. A party from *Fame* got aboard her and were able
to spend five minutes in the control room gathering papers before
hurriedly escaping as *U353* took her last plunge.

It was fortunate that the dogged defence and the arrival of air
escort had by this time discouraged the wolf-pack, for the last
remaining destroyer of the escort was now put out of action. *Fame*
had suffered an ugly tear in her hull along the water-line from the
U-boat's sharp hydroplanes. Her after magazine was flooded and
her stem was badly buckled. As she limped away, Lieutenant-
Commander C. A. Monsen, R.N.N., of the *Potentilla,* became senior
officer of the four corvettes left to defend the convoy. Had a further
concentrated attack been attempted it might have gone hard with
the convoy. As it was there was only one more encounter in which
the *Potentilla,* following up a radar contact, met a U-boat head-on
steering for the convoy. As the two ships raced by on opposite
courses, the corvette's 4-inch gun scored several hits and her depth-
charges were bursting round the submarine as she dived. The strong
smell of oil which lingered behind raised hopes that another of the
enemy could be counted destroyed to offset the losses in the convoy.
Though it was not so, the long fight was over. Against the grievous
loss of seven merchantmen and their valuable cargoes, two U-boats
had been sunk and a number damaged.

10

The Climax

So the Battle of the Atlantic lay still in the balance. From the German point of view U-boat losses were by no means insupportable. Merchant ships were being sunk at a rate greater than they could be replaced. On the other hand, by far the greater number of these were still ships out of convoy, and the convoy system was constantly being extended. These convoys were receiving improved protection, not only by stronger, better equipped and trained escort groups but, at least as important, by the very long-range Liberator aircraft which were at last being supplied, in increasing numbers, to squadrons of Coastal Command.

That a climax in the Atlantic was approaching, was clear. Karl Dönitz was not optimistic as to its outcome. He quotes from his War Diary for the 21st August, 1942, that 'these ever-increasing difficulties which confront us in the conduct of the war can only lead, in the normal course of events, to high, and indeed intolerable losses'. To counter this situation, urgent measures to improve the U-boats' equipment and weapons were put in hand. A search receiver, which picked up radar signals and warned the submarine commander that he had been detected, was produced and fitted. The development of a submarine with a high submerged speed was pressed ahead urgently. A torpedo which could 'home' acoustically on to the sound waves emanating from a ship's propellers was being experimented with as a weapon with which to hit back at escorts. The search receiver was not greatly to affect the issue as it was designed to pick up the transmissions of the early, $1\frac{1}{2}$-metre radar and was useless against the 10-centimetre radar which, unknown to the Germans, was being increasingly fitted in warships and aircraft. The new-type submarine and the acoustic torpedo were eventually to be very effective, but the issue was in fact to be decided before they were ready to enter the battle.

Dönitz's chief pre-occupation at this time was the increasing amount of air escort being given to the convoys and the shrinking gap in mid-Atlantic, where alone his U-boat commanders could operate without the constant fear of being surprised on the surface by aircraft which now carried highly lethal depth-charges. How right he was in his foreboding will be seen later. Even at this time, the closing months of 1942, when the Allied very long-range aircraft, still numbering only 10, had not yet perfected their technique and skill, it was being demonstrated how the provision of air escort, even only for a few hours, at the crisis of a convoy battle could turn the scales. The onset of a concentrated submarine attack inevitably disorganised the defence as individual escorts became detached chasing or hunting an enemy or rescuing survivors. Air escort, by harassing other attackers working their way in through the depleted surface escort, disorganised and delayed the attack while the defensive screen was reforming.

Meanwhile, as the wild Atlantic winter set in with the steady succession of cyclones sweeping across the convoy routes, whipping up monstrous seas, the intensity of the conflict flagged. Although two U-boat groups were always on station in the North Atlantic and achieved some success, much of Dönitz's force was widely dispersed. At first, seeking soft spots in the Allied defence, submarines were sent to the Trinidad area, where the convoy system had been slow in establishing itself, and to the waters off South Africa, where anti-submarine forces were weak and ill-organised. In both areas the submarines had considerable success without serious losses.

Then came the Allied landings in North Africa early in November 1942. Taken completely by surprise, the German High Command had failed to order U-boat dispositions to intercept the huge troop and supply convoys which thronged the Atlantic in the last half of October. The submarine group which might have done so was fully occupied in decimating the weakly escorted convoy from Freetown mentioned in the previous chapter. Thus the far more important convoys for North Africa arrived unscathed. Too late, Dönitz directed his boats to the Moroccan coast, the Straits of Gibraltar and the Western Mediterranean. They found no shortage of targets, but the convoys were strongly defended. In achieving a few successes the U-boats lost seven of their number in the space of a single week. The lesson was quickly absorbed by Admiral Dönitz. He correctly divined that to provide such strong escorts the Allies must have had to denude the regular trans-Atlantic convoys, the theatre in which Dönitz never ceased to insist that his boats could deliver a decisive blow. Ordered to send more boats into the Mediterranean to make good losses and to maintain 20 boats west of Gibraltar and Morocco, he protested that it 'would have disastrous effects on the war against shipping in the Atlantic, which U-boat Command has always regarded, and still regards, as the primary task of the U-boat arm. . . . This is a question of decisive importance.'

Dönitz's plea was disregarded. 1943 thus opened on a comparatively quiet note. During January only 15 ships were lost out of convoys in all areas. Yet indications emerged even from the few engagements, fought out amidst tempestuous weather, that the crisis of the battle was approaching. The Monthly Anti-Submarine report for that month, compiled in the Admiralty, contained the prophetic comment that 'a bolder and more reckless strategy is now characteristic of the enemy. The tempo is quickening and the critical phase of the U-boat war in the Atlantic cannot long be postponed.' In February, 34 ships in convoy were sunk, representing 14 per cent of the ships in convoys attacked. Against this, 12 submarines were sunk in the Atlantic, a rate of exchange which must have given Dönitz unpalatable food for thought.

Many convoys were crossing the Atlantic both ways in close succession without loss. Admiral Dönitz was disturbed and puzzled by the failure of his wide-spread patrol lines to find them. That it was partly owing to the Admiralty's uncannily accurate knowledge of his dispositions he knew. Able at this time to decypher British signals, he received the Admiralty's daily signalled 'U-boat Situation Report'. Thus he realised that to some extent the convoys were being diverted from danger areas by long-range control. What was not clear to him was that, in addition to this, the better-trained and equipped escort groups, in conjunction with air escort, by efficient use of H/F D/F and radar were often preventing the U-boats nearest to their route from closing to sight and report the convoy for which the wolf-pack was searching. A submarine forced to dive by a patrolling aircraft might be held down for the crucial period during which the convoy was passing through the patrol line. At other times accurate knowledge of the position of the shadowing submarine would enable an escort commander to detach a pair of ships to hunt it, keeping it down and perhaps destroying or damaging it. Meanwhile the convoy would make a drastic alteration of course, leaving the converging wolf-pack to cast vainly in the wrong direction. What, in fact, Dönitz could not know was that the escort forces were reaching a state of efficiency such as his wolf-packs had never previously experienced.

In November 1942, Admiral Sir Percy Noble had come to the end of his term of office as Commander-in-Chief, Western Approaches. In the period since the 17th February, 1941, when he had taken up the appointment, tremendous advances had been made, not simply in the strength of the forces he had been able to gather to throw into the battle but also in their organisation, equipment and training. Under constant pressure to release his personnel, officers and men, experienced in the specialised form of warfare around the convoys, for the superficially more important tasks of manning the new ships going to swell the fleets in other theatres, he had yet succeeded in largely keeping together the trained escort groups which experience had shown to be essential. Bases for them had been built up from nothing at Liverpool, Greenock and Londonderry, where the storm-battered ships were taken in hand for maintenance and repairs between voyages and their crews underwent the intensive training so necessary to keep them at a peak of efficiency, with a knowledge of the latest weapons and tactics.

Thus when his successor, Admiral Sir Max Horton, took over he found in his hand the weapon with which he was to win one of the most clear-cut and decisive victories of the war. Though Max Horton will be remembered as the victor in the Battle of the Atlantic, Percy Noble can justly claim to have been the architect of that victory. A school, known as the Western Approaches Tactical Unit, had been set up in Liverpool in February 1942 to give synthetic training to escort captains and group commanders in the tactics of convoy battles. It had done much to instil a common doctrine of convoy defence, together with the team spirit and initiative which were the mark of a well-trained escort group. In January 1943, to this theoretical type of training was added practical application at sea of the lessons learnt, by the institution of a school housed in Mr. Tom Sopwith's steam yacht, serving the Royal Navy as H.M.S. *Philante*, to which were attached a number of training submarines. Before setting out with their convoys, escort groups would be given intensive practice under the guidance, firstly of Captain A. J. Baker-Cresswell and later of Captain L. F. Durnford-Slater, both experienced escort commanders, and a staff of specialist officers.

In these ways the quality of the escort groups was raised and kept at a high level. Their numbers were at the same time being increased. Whereas up to this time there had been a permanent shortage of escorts, resulting in convoys being weakly defended, it now became possible not only to increase the size of escorts, from an average of five and a half to seven and a half for each convoy, and to allow time between voyages for this essential training, but also to begin the formation of Support Groups—reserve groups which could be sent to reinforce the regular escorts when a convoy was threatened or was passing through a concentration of U-boats. This had been for a long time an agreed requirement, but shortage of suitable ships and experienced captains had prevented its adoption.

The emergence of the necessary surplus came about largely as a result of the labours of scientists engaged on operational research under Professor P. M. S. Blackett, who had gone to the Admiralty in January 1942 after nine months work for Coastal Command. In the autumn of that year, by statistical examination of the battle figures up to that time, Operational Research deduced a number of facts of which perhaps the most important, because it could not otherwise become apparent, was that, whereas the number of ships lost in a convoy battle depended, as might be expected, upon the number of U-boats attacking and the size of the escort, it was quite independent of the size of convoy. Thus by increasing the size of convoys from an average of 32 ships to 54, which reduced the *numbers* of convoys open to attack at any one time, losses could be lessened by 56 per cent.

The results of taking such a step would be cumulative. They would firstly enable more escorts, air as well as surface, to be allocated to each convoy. Statistics showed that by increasing the number of escorts from six to nine, losses would be reduced by 25 per cent, whereas, if air escort could be supplied for eight hours each day, the reduction would be no less than 64 per cent. The apparent objection that the value of larger escorts would be offset by the larger area to be defended was met by the elementary mathematical fact that, whereas the area of a convoy is proportional to the square of its dimensions, the length of perimeter to be occupied by the escorts is proportionate only to the length of the radius. Secondly, an increase in the number of escorts might enable an escort commander to station them in a double ring round the convoy thus achieving a defence in depth. Furthermore, he would be able to go over to the offensive more readily as he could afford to detach hunting sections more frequently and allow them to stay away longer, without too seriously reducing the screen round the convoy. Then, as has been said, the economy of force, achieved by reducing the number of convoys to be defended, provided a surplus of warships which could be formed into Support Groups. These in themselves resulted in a further economy. For, provided that the convoy escort could be reinforced during the passage of the most dangerous areas, a smaller escort could safely be given for the remainder of the convoy's voyage. Thus Operational Research, too often neglected or ignored, was responsible for a revolution in organisation, which came about in March 1943 with an adjustment of the North Atlantic convoy cycle, whereby fewer and larger convoys were sailed each way.

The startling forecast of a 64 per cent reduction of losses in convoy which would be achieved by a regular provision of air escort was not, however, given its due weight. The limited number of Liberator aircraft, which were adaptable for the very long range work necessary for the purpose, were coveted by Bomber Command of the R.A.F., who had the backing of the Air Staff in their belief that priority had to be given to a maximum bombing effort on Germany. Furthermore, a number of those available to Coastal Command were employed on unproductive patrolling of the U-boat's transit areas—between Iceland and the Hebrides and in the Bay of Biscay. Consequently at the turn of the year there were still no more than 10 V.L.R. Liberator aircraft able to operate in mid-Atlantic. Yet this handful of aircraft was time and again to intervene decisively in convoy battles, while the number of U-boats sunk by aircraft on the 'defensive' work of convoy escort was far in excess of those which were destroyed on 'offensive' patrols. In the nine months from June 1942 to March 1943, while aircraft operating as air escorts or in direct support of convoys in the North Atlantic destroyed 22 enemy submarines, the 'Bay Offensive', which involved 3,500 patrol hours each month and the loss of some 100 aircraft, accounted for only seven.

After the withdrawal of the U-boat packs from the North Atlantic convoy routes at the end of May 1943 which, together with the presence of aircraft-carriers with the convoys, released many of the shore-based aircraft from escort duty, it was possible to saturate the Bay of Biscay with aircraft. Even so it was only a tactical error by the enemy that led to a temporary achievement of worthwhile results. The inability of the U-boats to detect transmissions from 10-centi-metre radar had led to a few of them being caught on the surface at night by aircraft and sunk or badly damaged. Dönitz therefore decided to increase the anti-aircraft armament of his boats, which were then sailed in groups and ordered to fight it out with the air-craft. These tactics were only momentarily successful. As soon as they were appreciated, a technique to defeat them was adopted. The first aircraft to come on the scene called up reinforcements. A synchronised attack was then delivered—with devastating results. Thus in June and July 1943 the Bay Offensive at last paid a worth-while dividend, 17 U-boats being sunk by aircraft in that area. When, on the 3rd August, 1943, the enemy reverted to independent sailings, surfacing only for the minimum time to recharge batteries, submarine losses on passage at once returned to the previous low rate, only four being destroyed in the three months following. So far as the rival claims of Bomber Command were concerned, Professor Blackett was able to show, as he recorded in an article in *Brassey's Annual* for 1953, that

> From the figures on the effectiveness of air cover, it could be calculated that a long-range Liberator operating from Iceland and escorting the convoys in the middle of the Atlantic *saved* at least half a dozen merchant ships in its service lifetime of some thirty flying sorties. If used for bombing Berlin, the same aircraft in its service life would drop less than 100 tons of bombs and kill not more than a couple of dozen enemy men, women and children and destroy a number of houses.
>
> No one would dispute that the saving of six merchant ships and their crews and cargoes was of incomparably more value to the Allied war effort than the killing of some two dozen enemy civilians, the destruction of a number of houses and a certain very small effect on production.
>
> The difficulty was to get the figures believed. But believed they eventually were and more long-range aircraft were made available to Coastal Command.

Nevertheless the Prime Minister's Anti-U-Boat Committee, examining the claims of the various contestants, achieved only a compromise which by March 1943 raised the number of V.L.R. aircraft from 10 to 40, allowing about 13 to be operational at any one time.

It was in March 1943 that an escort aircraft-carrier, the U.S.S. *Bogue*, made its first appearance with a trans-Atlantic convoy. British ships of this type had been operating for some time; but, though they were intended to give convoys the continuous anti-submarine air escort which experience was soon to prove would give them almost complete immunity from submarine attack, they had at first been diverted to take part in the North African landings. There they had performed valuable service in providing fighter cover for the fleet until fighters of the Royal Air Force were able to establish themselves on airfields ashore. It was not to be until April 1943, therefore, that these ships were able to take up their pre-destined role and supply one of the most important ingredients of the victory about to be won. Similarly it was not until April that the advantages accruing from the changes in the convoy cycle were to be fully enjoyed, particularly in the shape of Support Groups. One of these was to be made up of an escort carrier and three destroyers and was to prove its great worth immediately.

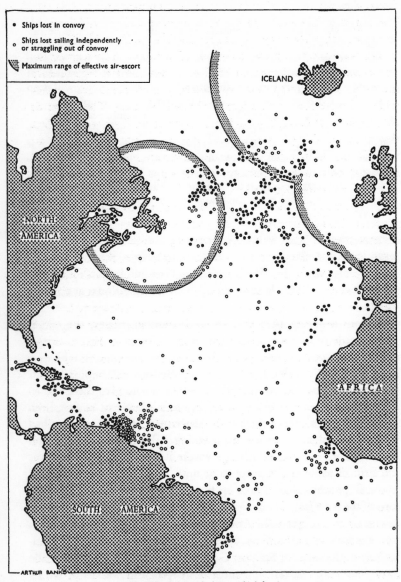

Ships lost in convoy

Ships lost sailing independently
or straggling out of convoy

Maximum range of effective air-escort

ICELAND

NORTH
AMERICA

AFRICA

SOUTH   AMERICA

ARTHUR BANKS

46 *The decisive clash in mid-Atlantic*
1st August, 1942 to 31st May, 1943

Nevertheless, March 1943 opened with brighter prospects in Allied view than ever before in the long-drawn Battle of the Atlantic. The majority of escort groups were imbued with a well-founded confidence that they were a match for the wolf-packs. Yet this month was in fact to prove to be one of the most disastrous of the war in terms of merchant shipping lost. It was the dark hour before the dawn. In the first 10 days of March, 41 ships were lost, world-wide; 56 more were to be lost in the next 10 days. These figures alone were not enough to indicate catastrophe. Nor was the fact that nearly two-thirds of this number were sunk in convoy; for, in fact, during March the submarines, swarming in unprecedented numbers, only sank 11 per cent of the ships in the convoys they attacked, a not insufferable loss rate.

It was two other factors which caused alarm to rise to the level of crisis. Three homeward-bound convoys, set upon by large concentrations of U-boats, lost no less than 34 of their number, at a cost to the enemy of only one submarine. Also only six of the enemy were destroyed by air or surface escorts round the convoys during the whole month. Thus, while the U-boats were accounting for 12 merchant ships for every one of their number destroyed, there seemed to be evidence that convoy defence was helpless against really massive concentrations of attackers. The first of these convoys to suffer was the slow, homeward-bound SC121. It was beset by every form of foul weather. A gale of wind, raising towering seas and driving a swirling blanket of snow before it in which the convoy became scattered, was followed by fog which made its re-assembly slow and difficult. Seventeen U-boats had doggedly pursued it through the storm. Some fell upon the stragglers and picked them off one by one. Others were able to get through the disorganised defence and sink more from the main body.

Some indications of how the U-boats were able to range freely amongst the ships of the convoy is given by the account of the master of the freighter *Kingswood*, Captain R. Coates, who describes how, in the darkness and the gale, as he peered anxiously out from his bridge, his eye was caught by what seemed to be a particularly heavy breaking sea on his port bow. Then he saw that the white flurry was travelling with some speed towards him. 'It's a torpedo', he shouted to the mate standing beside him. But almost at once he realised that he was in fact looking at the wash of a submarine travelling at high speed on the surface. He ran to the telegraph and gave a double ring, calling for utmost emergency speed and steered to ram. 'I really felt we could not miss,' he recorded.

> Collision seemed inevitable. About this time I heard the U-boat's engine and a voice in the distance. I was sort of hanging on waiting for the crash when I saw the submarine's wake curling round—the voice I had heard must have been the U-boat's commander shouting 'Hard a Port' in German. The submarine's wake curled right under my stem —how its tail missed us I still do not know.

The ship's 4-inch gun and machine guns let fly at the conning-tower but the submarine vanished quickly into the night to seek other victims.

Thirteen ships were sent to the bottom from SC121 without loss to the attackers. Yet, at about the same time, another group of U-boats, falling in with the east-bound convoy from Halifax, HX228, meeting a better organised and more resolute defence, lost two of their number while sinking only four of the convoy and a destroyer. The destroyer *Harvester* was commanded by Commander A. A. Tait, senior officer of a group of British, Polish and Free French escorts, one of the groups which had reached a high state of efficiency under their experienced leader. Running down a radar contact, Tait sighted *U444* on the surface and rammed her. This usually most effective and certain way of destroying a submarine had its dangers, however. As the *Harvester* drove through and over, the submarine scraped and bumped its way along the destroyer's keel and became wedged under her propellers. The two vessels lay locked in this way for a time, and, by the time the U-boat finally broke free, *Harvester*'s propellers and shafts had suffered so much damage that she was reduced to a slow crawl on one engine.

The French corvette *Aconit*, coming to her leader's help, found *U444* still miraculously afloat and delivered the *coup de grâce* by ramming her again. Meanwhile, Tait, in spite of *Harvester*'s heavy damage, had rescued 50 survivors from one of the sunken merchant ships before limping slowly on. *Aconit* was ordered away to rejoin the convoy; but soon after daylight *Harvester*'s propeller shaft

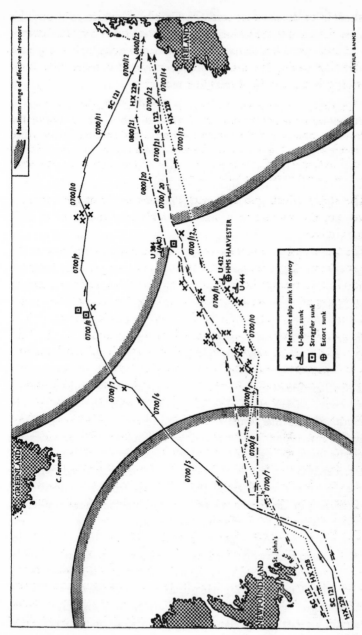

ARTHUR BANKS

47 The passage of four convoys during March 1943, the critical period of the battle

cracked, bringing her to a standstill. Called back again to *Harvester*'s aid, *Aconit* was still some distance away when a column of smoke on the horizon and a last signal told Lieutenant Levasseur, her captain, that the helpless and immobilised destroyer had been torpedoed. Hurrying to the rescue, *Aconit* was rewarded with an asdic contact. Depth-charges brought a U-boat to the surface and once again Levasseur had the satisfaction of ramming and sinking one of the enemy—a satisfaction deepened by the discovery that his victim, *U432*, had been responsible for torpedoing the *Harvester*. Loss of life from *Harvester* was tragically heavy, and included her captain. But this drawn battle had again showed that a first-class escort group could hold the wolf-packs at bay and make them pay heavily for any successes.

Besides the two submarines destroyed, at least one other very nearly suffered the same fate. *U121* was responsible for two of the merchant ships sunk. One of them, carrying explosives, blew up. Débris crashed against the U-boat's periscope, damaging it. While thus blinded, Korvetten-Kapitän Trojer, the submarine's captain, heard the thrash of a destroyer's propeller. As he took his boat down in a crash dive, depth-charges exploded round her, causing the conning-tower hatch to leak, letting a mass of water into her. *U121* escaped destruction by going deep but it was a very narrow escape.

The other side of the coin was to be seen when the next two home-ward convoys, HX229 and SC122, met the U-boat swarm in mid-Atlantic. The former, with a weak and ill-assorted escort gathered together at random, was set upon by 38 U-boats where no air escort could be given. No rescue ship having been included in the convoy, the escort was at once faced, when the attack developed, with the bitter choice between leaving the survivors from torpedoed ships to their fate or disorganising and weakening the already quite in-adequate defence. The dilemma was an insoluble one and, in the course of two days, 13 ships of the convoy were sent to the bottom.

HX229 had meanwhile been overhauling the slow SC122. As the two convoys drew close to each other the attack was extended to them both. SC122 had a regular group of reasonable strength but it was swamped by the weight of the attack and lost eight ships. Liberator aircraft from Iceland joined the defence on the second day, and the resultant harassment of the U-boats, culminating in the destruction of one of them, finally brought the battle to a close. Although Admiral Dönitz records that 'nearly all the other boats suffered from depth-charges or bombs and two were severely damaged', it was a clear victory for the attackers.

As the mounting tale of convoy losses reached the Admiralty something approaching dismay or even despair developed. Voices were raised questioning whether the virtue had gone out of the convoy system. To quote from Captain Roskill's official history, *The War at Sea*, the Naval Staff were later to record that 'the Germans never came so near to disrupting communications between the New World and the Old as in the first twenty days of March 1943', and 'it appeared possible that we should not be able to continue [to regard] convoy as an effective form of defence'. This was tantamount to an admission of defeat. For there was no possible alternative, as a glance at the record of ships sailed independently made abundantly clear. Disastrous as were the stories of a few of the trans-Atlantic convoys at this time, many others were being brought or fought through relatively unscathed, so that the total losses represented no more than 2·5 per cent of the ships sailed in convoy. Even considering the convoys which were attacked, the losses were only 11 per cent. Independently sailing ships, on the other hand, suffered a loss rate more than double that of convoys, while independents which came under actual attack lost no less than 80 per cent of their number.

In fact a set-back on one part of the battlefield was being unreasonably looked upon as a herald of general defeat. The crisis passed. As March gave way to April the escort forces were gathering their strength to deliver the knock-out blow.

I I

Victory

March 1943, with its grim tale of convoy losses, shook the Admiralty's confidence in the future prospects of the Battle of the Atlantic. And indeed from the comparatively detached viewpoint of Whitehall this was perhaps natural. Those closer to the fighting, however, such as the commander-in-chief, Western Approaches, and his staff at Liverpool, the captains commanding the escort bases and the escort commanders themselves were by no means so dismayed. They were better able to appreciate the results to be expected from the imminent arrival on the scene of the special Support Groups, of the escort carriers which provided continuous, direct air escort and of increased numbers of shore-based, long-range aircraft. Even without these reinforcements, some of the escort groups, particularly those with a high proportion of destroyers in their composition, were demonstrating on trip after trip, that, by efficient use of the equipment and weapons now available, even powerful concentrations of U-boats could be held off while the convoys passed on their way unscathed or with very minor losses.

Already, before the month of March was out, the tide of battle had begun to turn. Following their success in mauling HX229 and SC122, as related in the previous chapter, fresh U-boat packs were concentrated to intercept the next two homeward-bound convoys. Though submarine patrol lines were correctly stationed and both convoys were intercepted, they were shepherded safely through without loss. First of all, the U-boat making initial contact was detected by H/F D/F, pounced upon, put down and held down so that the wolf-packs, deprived of a shadower to guide them to their prey, were prevented or delayed from concentrating round them;

then, a Support Group was brought in to reinforce the convoy escorts through the danger area; and finally, as the convoys came within range of air escort from Iceland, the long-range Liberators so harassed the pursuing U-boats that they were forced to withdraw, empty-handed. This combination of efficient use of the improved weapons available to the convoy escorts—H/F D/F, 10-centimetre radar and the latest asdic sets—of reinforcement in the danger area and of close co-operation with shore-based aircraft, now also fitted with 10-centimetre radar, was the classic form of defence at last perfected and was the basis on which victory was to be won. It was to be made more certain by the imminent addition of the escort aircraft-carrier which would abolish the mid-Atlantic gap in air cover.

The turn of the tide of battle was somewhat obscured at this time, however, by conflicting cross-currents. During the last 11 days of March only 15 ships were lost in the North Atlantic compared with the dreadful total of 107 during the previous three weeks; but this period was one of tempestuous weather in which the storms normal in that time of year rose to the intensity of hurricanes. Merchantmen, escorts and submarines were alike too absorbed in a struggle for survival to give much thought for the enemy. Whether eastward-bound, deeply laden and with deck cargoes of landing-craft, lorries or tanks, which often made them crank dangerously, or west-bound in ballast, riding high, with their screws thrashing on the surface, the merchant ships were forced to heave-to and concentrate on their own safety. Convoys became widely scattered. The Commodore's ship of one of them capsized and was lost with all hands. The little ships of the escort force climbed the steep sides of the monstrous waves and hung momentarily poised on their crests with bow and stern out of water before plunging dizzily down the farther slopes. For hour after hour this process repeated itself. Damage mounted, hull plates splitting, rivets shaking loose, boats being smashed, men swept overboard and the delicate electric and electronic anti-submarine devices put out of order. The German submarines, though they had proved their staunchness and sea-keeping qualities in three North Atlantic winters, found themselves similarly reduced to a single-minded struggle with the elements. Admiral Dönitz quotes from the log of *U260* which in these conditions came across a merchant ship running before the gale and attempted to attack her:

> *2200.* Pursuit broken off. While trying to run before the storm at full speed, the boat dived twice. By blowing tanks, putting my helm hard over and reducing speed I managed to hold her reasonably well on the surface. To remain on the bridge was impossible. Within half an hour the captain and the watch were half-drowned. Five tons of water poured into the boat in no time through the conning tower hatch, the voice-pipe and the diesel ventilating shaft. . . . With a heavy heart I abandoned the chase.

Thus, for a time both sides turned to face a common enemy. The new trend in the Battle was also obscured during the last days of March and the first half of April 1943 by a temporary reduction in the number of U-boats at sea. Those which had taken part in the big battles of mid-March had returned to base to re-arm and re-fuel. Only one group was stationed at the beginning of April on the trans-Atlantic routes. This intercepted HX231 which was escorted by one of the 'First Division' teams, led by Commander Peter Gretton. The reception awaiting any wolf-pack which accepted combat with a well-escorted convoy was demonstrated. Though handicapped by having only one destroyer, only one ship fitted with H/F D/F and by the absence of a rescue ship, Gretton's team, helped by good co-operation by Liberator aircraft from Iceland, beat off a concentrated attack, losing only three ships at a cost to the enemy of two of his submarines and others severely damaged, a rate of exchange the Germans could by no means afford. Unfortunately this satisfactory result was obscured by the loss of three more ships which had belonged to the convoy. One had dropped behind with engine trouble, while two foreign ships, a Dutchman and a Swede, broke convoy at the first attack and paid the inevitable penalty.

Yet even such a repulse of the wolf-packs, satisfactory as it seemed in a cold, statistical light, had to be paid for in harsh, human tragedy of the kind which runs through the whole story of the Battle of the Atlantic. Lack of space in a book of this kind and a necessary avoidance of repetitive narrative prevents much reference to it; but it should not be forgotten. The absence of a rescue ship placed the escort commander in an agonising dilemma. It was familiar to all engaged in convoy defence. Commander Gretton has described it on this occasion:

> The unfortunate ship which had been hit was loaded with iron ore and sank within two minutes. Searching for the U-boat, we passed survivors who were scattered in the icy water, each with his red light burning. Some were on rafts, some were alone, but no boats had survived. It is my most painful memory of the war that we had to shout encouragement, knowing well that it was unlikely that they would ever be picked up.
>
> It was an appalling decision to have to make, to stop or go on: but by leaving her place in the search, the ship would leave a gap through which more attacks could be made and more men drowned. We had to go on. After a search plan had been completed I sent back the *Pink* to look for survivors but she failed to find them and after four hours' search I had to recall her to her station. . . .
>
> I could not stop thinking of the men in the water astern and only after the report of the next attack had come in was I able to achieve proper concentration again.

Meanwhile the temporary U-boat vacuum in the North Atlantic was being rapidly filled by a stream of fresh U-boats from Germany and from the Biscay bases. No less than 98 sailed during the month. Dönitz could no longer complain that his forces were being diverted from the main target. But their lack of success was a warning of what was to come.

Gathering round HX233, escorted by the mixed American and British group led by Commander Paul Heinemann, U.S.N., in the Coastguard Cutter *Spencer*, they succeeded in torpedoing only one ship, while *U176* was destroyed by the *Spencer*'s depth-charges in return. This convoy had taken a route more southerly than usual and operations took place in calm, blue weather. Dönitz ascribed the lack of success to these conditions. The U-boat Command War Diary for the 18th April, 1943 commented, 'Meagre success, achieved generally, at the cost of heavy losses, renders operations in these areas inadvisable.' There was more to it than that, however. His boats, moved north and stationed athwart the route of the slow outward-bound convoys ONS3 and ONS4, found themselves unable to build up any concentration against them. ONS4 was supported by H.M.S. *Biter*, the first British escort carrier to operate on the trans-Atlantic routes. The close escort, one of the most experienced British groups, led by the destroyer *Hesperus*, shepherded the convoy unharmed through the first patrol line encountered, sinking *U191*, the boat which made contact. The second patrol line was similarly thrust through. The boat which made contact was pin-pointed by H/F D/F from the close escort, attacked and driven down by aircraft from the *Biter* and then destroyed by the *Pathfinder*, one of the carrier's screen. The convoy sailed on, more in peril from the swarm of icebergs through which it was routed than from the frustrated enemy.

The last week in April, indeed, constituted the first real signs that the tide of victory had set in the Allies' favour in the Battle of the Atlantic, five U-boats being destroyed round the convoys for almost negligible loss of merchant ships. Before defeat could be turned into rout, however, one final destructive clash had to be experienced. It took place around convoy ONS5 escorted by Peter Gretton's group. It was a small convoy of about 40 ships, mostly elderly tramps of uncertain reliability and speeds—for every ship which floated was being pressed into Atlantic service at this time, to replace the heavy losses of the last 12 months and to speed the build-up in England of vast quantities of munitions and equipment being gathered for the great enterprise of Normandy. The ocean escort, which formed up round the convoy as it passed through the North Channel on 22nd April, 1943, comprised Gretton's own ship, the destroyer *Duncan*, the frigate *Tay*, one of a new class of escorts, and four corvettes, *Sunflower*, *Loosestrife*, *Snowflake* and *Pink*. Another destroyer, the *Vidette*, had gone ahead to Iceland to escort three ships to join the convoy. ONS5 went through almost every experience possible for an Atlantic convoy. In the course of them it progressed through harsh tribulation to eventual triumph. Its story is worth telling for that reason as well as because it has been judged the turning point in the Battle of the Atlantic.

The northerly route the convoy had been given, which would take it up into the region of almost constant gales, as well as the venerable appearance and light loading of many of its ships, gave warning to the escort commander of difficulties ahead. Heavy weather would reduce the sluggish pace to a crawl. Some ships would be brought to a standstill, others would fall out of control. It was not long before forebodings became fact. As the convoy plugged its way north-westward, the corvettes were kept busy shepherding stray sheep back into the fold and escorting stragglers who were trying to catch up the main body. During one wild night of tempest, two ships collided and one of them was so damaged that she had to be detached to Iceland for repairs. The convoy Commodore, Captain J. Brooks, R.N.R., could at one time count no less than eight of his ships showing the 'two red lights vertical' of a ship not under control.

Nevertheless, by the 27th, when the gale at last took off somewhat, only the damaged ship and one other which had been detached as too slow were missing. The improvement in the weather also eased Gretton's mind for the time being with regard to that constant anxiety of a sea commander, fuel for his destroyers. The *Duncan* had not been modified like other old destroyers, including the *Vidette*, to carry extra oil fuel by the removal of one boiler. Her endurance was very inadequate for long convoy voyages. Unless she could replenish from time to time from the specially fitted tanker she would be unable to remain with the convoy much beyond the longitude of Iceland. Now, however, both the *Duncan* and the *Vidette*, which had joined with the Iceland contingent the day before, were able to refill their oil tanks.

It was none too soon. Early on the 28th April the most northerly of a U-boat group, widely spread on a patrol line running north and south across the convoy routes, caught sight of the convoy. A report was at once on the air to U-boat Command, whence orders sending the whole U-boat pack in pursuit were sent out. Picked up by the H/F D/F operators in the escorts, it also served to warn them that the convoy was being shadowed. The brief easement of the weather had passed. Low cloud scudding across a stormy sea prevented any air escort operating. The surface escorts could steam at only moderate speeds which reduced their ability to break up or scare away the gathering pack. However, shortly before dark, taking *Duncan* and *Tay* out in the direction in which a transmission had been detected, Gretton sighted the cloud of spray thrown up by a U-boat travelling on the surface. In the prevailing conditions the asdic failed to make contact with the submarine after it had dived, but *Tay* was left to keep it down until dark.

The threat to the convoy had been quickly appreciated at Western Approaches Headquarters. R.A.F. Coastal Command were called upon for help. Catalina flying-boats from Iceland were despatched. South of the convoy they caught three U-boats heading northwards on the surface. Swooping to the attack they forced them to dive, putting them out of the chase and seriously damaging one of them. Nevertheless, the night which followed was one of repeated efforts by several other U-boats to insinuate their way through the screen of escorts. Six times radar contact was made with them, by the *Duncan* on four separate occasions and once each by *Sunflower* and *Snowflake*. On each occasion the submarine was chased and forced to dive, but in the rising gale and heavy seas, with the ships rolling gunwales under, decks awash and spray flying mast-high, the encounters were inconclusive.

The attempted attacks were foiled. Dawn revealed an undepleted convoy thrusting slowly westwards into steep seas under a lowering grey sky. The wolf-pack, discouraged by the night's events, had given up the chase for the time being and, on orders from U-boat Command, had set off south-westwards to join another group lying in wait far ahead on the convoy's expected route—all except one submarine. This one had attained a good position ahead and, lying submerged, was waiting for his targets to approach. In spite of the difficult weather and the tumbled sea, her commander succeeded in delivering an attack, torpedoing one ship. The escorts at once carried out the pre-arranged search plan for such an occasion but without success. The loss was a mortifying experience after the effective defence put up during the night. However, it was the only one to result from this first encounter with the wolf-pack. For the next five days it was the weather which constituted the enemy to be faced as the wind rose steadily. By the evening of the 30th April it was blowing a full gale from the south-west. The 'merry month of May' opened for the convoy in winds of hurricane force and mountainous seas whose crests were whipped off in a solid sheet of spray, reducing visibility to a few hundred yards. The low-powered, lightly loaded tramp steamers of the convoy, riding high out of the water, forced to heave to, could concentrate only on their own safety, while the convoy began to disintegrate. Two ships ran for shelter to Iceland. The remainder became widely scattered. Not until the 2nd May did the wind take off sufficiently for the escorts, aided by a Liberator aircraft which had come out from Iceland, to set about gathering their flock together again. It was none too soon. For ahead, stretching across the route, was the edge of the great field of icebergs which come drifting south from the Arctic at this time of year. The merchantmen were concentrated into three groups: 20 ships with the Commodore forming the main body, 10 more being brought to join it under escort of the *Tay*, while some 50 miles astern were six more ships with the *Pink*.

An equally serious aspect of the tumultuous weather conditions and, in the event, of greater consequence, was the impossibility of refuelling destroyers. The *Oribi*, of the 3rd Support Group, had joined the escort three days earlier and, in a brief easement of the weather on the 30th April, had been able to top up her tanks. But before others of the escort could do the same the gale had descended again. By the 3rd May, the *Duncan* was critically short of fuel and in the afternoon of that day had to leave the convoy and make directly for St. John's, Newfoundland, where she arrived with tanks almost empty. The duty of Senior Officer of the Escort devolved upon the captain of the *Tay*, Lieutenant-Commander R. E. Sherwood, R.N.R. His detached group of merchantmen had by this time joined the main body, increasing its number to 30. *Pink* and her stragglers were still far behind.

Meanwhile the convoy was heading for the heavy concentration of U-boats spread across the route. The Admiralty's U-boat tracking organisation had made the Commander-in-Chief, Western Approaches, well aware of the impending threat. A diversion to avoid it was impossible. Reinforcement for the escort in the shape of four more destroyers of the 3rd Support Group, *Offa, Penn, Panther* and *Impulsive*, had joined during the 2nd May. But by the 4th May *Penn*, *Panther* and *Impulsive* had also reached the end of their endurance and were forced to seek harbour to refuel. Hardly had they gone, leaving the escort of the main body consisting of three destroyers and four corvettes, when the first indications of the enemy's approach were received by the H/F D/F operators. From every direction the wolves were gathering. First blood was to be to the defence, however. The convoy was by now within range of air cover from Newfoundland. Though fog over the air bases reduced the air effort to a few sorties only, a Canso aircraft of the Royal Canadian Air Force surprised $U630$ on the surface that evening and despatched it with a well-placed 'stick' of depth-charges.

During the day, with the weather at last calming down, the U-boats, more than 30 of them, gathered round. As night fell, they moved in to the attack. The first to suffer was a straggler, six miles astern of the main body. For the next 24 hours attack after attack succeeded in getting through, and, by the evening of the 6th May, 11 ships of the convoy had been sent to the bottom. Though the escorts had again and again detected and driven off attackers, the defence was swamped by sheer numbers. The situation by the evening of the 5th seemed indeed desperate. The senior officer of the 3rd Support Group can be excused for recording at the time that 'the convoy seemed doomed to certain annihilation'. But in fact the dogged, unwearying defence was about to turn the tables. It was aided by the descent of the fog which so often follows an Atlantic storm. Already two U-boats had been sunk. The first had been $U630$ as recorded above. Then, during the forenoon of the 5th, the corvette *Pink*, commanded by Lieutenant Robert Atkinson, R.N.R., still shepherding her little group of stragglers, gained asdic contact with a U-boat shaping up for an attack. The *Pink*'s depth-charges pounded the submarine, later identified as $U192$, to destruction.

The U-boat losses were already such as to make the result so far no better for the enemy than a drawn battle. As the fog settled down the escort's advantage by reason of their excellent radar became paramount. They took full advantage of it. As Lieutenant-Commander Sherwood reported later, 'All ships showed dash and initiative. No ship required to be told what to do and signals were distinguished both by their brevity and wit.' These were the marks of the well-trained escort group. No less than twenty-four attempts to penetrate the defensive screen during the night of the 5th/6th May were defeated. In the course of these encounters, $U638$, caught on the surface by the corvette *Loosestrife*. Lieutenant Stonehouse,

R.N.R., was blown up by a pattern of depth-charges as she was diving. The *Vidette,* commanded by Lieutenant Raymond Hart, detecting a submerged submarine, delivered an attack with her Hedgehog. It was later established that the explosions which followed marked the destruction of *U125.* Two more submarines were to follow her before dawn. Lieutenant-Commander J. C. A. Ingram of the *Oribi,* surprising *U531* in the fog, rammed and cut her down. Finally, Commander Godfrey Brewer of the *Pelican,* bringing his 1st Support Group to reinforce the convoy escort, depth-charged *U438* to destruction.

With daylight on the 6th May the battle round ONS5 came to an end as the shaken and demoralised survivors of the U-boat pack withdrew. As many as 60 U-boats in all had been directed to join the attack. Twelve merchant ships were sunk at the cost to the enemy of six of their number destroyed by surface and air escorts. Two others, running through the night in chase, had collided and gone down. A number of others had narrowly escaped destruction and been badly damaged. Such an exchange, as Admiral Dönitz has recorded, constituted a defeat for the U-boats. As the losses became known and the stories of survivors, surprised on the surface again and again and barely escaping destruction, spread through the U-boat Command, morale plunged. Re-directed to the homeward-bound convoys HX237 and SC129, the U-boats displayed a marked reluctance to move in to attack.

HX237 was strongly escorted, having the inestimable benefit of continuous air escort by aircraft from *Biter* as well as of shore-based aircraft. Three ships were lost from the convoy but at the cost of three U-boats. SC129, on the other hand, was beset by a strong group of submarines, losing two merchant ships at the outset. Thereafter, however, the surface escort of two destroyers and four corvettes had no difficulty in keeping the attackers at bay, *U186* being sunk by the destroyer *Hesperus* and several others being severely damaged. Commenting on this action, Dönitz quotes from his War Diary:

> No less than eleven of the boats in contact with the convoy were detected and driven off while it was still light. This is a very high percentage. It is obvious that the enemy must have detected all the

boats in contact with astonishing certainty. . . . Since detection on this scale and with such promptitude has hitherto been unknown, the possibility that the enemy is using a new and efficient type of locating device cannot be ruled out.

It was true, of course, that the existence of an efficient, ship-borne H/F D/F was not known to the Germans. The submarines consequently had no inhibitions about use of radio and each transmission was apt to result in the appearance from over the horizon of an aircraft or a surface escort accurately directed on to the transmitter. On the other hand when, as in the case of SC129, it was usually only a Flower-class corvette which could be spared for the purpose, the U-boats with their higher turn of speed had little to fear. In days gone by they would have treated it with contempt. But now the empty gesture of defiance by the escorts was enough to induce the enemy to 'throw in the sponge'. The moral superiority achieved by the escorts was unmistakable. The Monthly Anti-Submarine Report for April, compiled in the Admiralty, contained the prophetic pronouncement:

> Historians of this war are likely to single out the months of April and May 1943 as the critical period during which strength began to ebb away from the German U-boat offensive, not because of the low figure of shipping sunk, not because of the satisfactory high number of U-boats destroyed, but because for the first time U-boats failed to press home attacks on convoys when favourably placed to do so.

The next homeward convoy to encounter the U-boat packs, SC130, made the picture even clearer. The escort was again Commander Gretton's group. Flushed with their previous triumph, they went gaily and confidently into action. Not a ship of the convoy was sunk while no less than five U-boats were destroyed, two by surface escorts and three by escorting aircraft. In one of them died Dönitz's son. The final discomfiture of the U-boat packs took place round convoy HX239 where aircraft from the United States carrier *Bogue* and from H.M.S. *Archer* drove off the submarines and sent two of them to the bottom on the 23rd May, 1943. Though the fiercely fought battle round ONS5, previously described, has come to be recognised as the final turning point in the Battle of the Atlantic, it was the almost total failure of the U-boats against the convoys

immediately following which marked their decisive defeat. As
Dönitz has written, 'The overwhelming superiority achieved by the
enemy defence was finally proved beyond dispute in the operations
against convoys SC130 and HX239.'

U-boat losses had indeed become a massacre. In the first 22 days
of May no less than 31 had been destroyed. For it was not only
round the convoys that they were now being sunk. Aircraft fitted
with 10-centimetre radar had at last been allocated to the anti-
submarine role in something approaching the numbers demanded
by the Admiralty. For the first time the 'Bay Offensive' against
submarines on passage to and from their bases on the French Atlantic
coast had begun to show a reasonable return for the effort involved,
six being sunk during May.

The reversal of fortune in the interval since the gloomy forebodings of the Admiralty in March was as complete as it was sudden.
By the end of May 41 U-boats had been sunk during the month. Of
these, 14 had fallen to the convoy surface escorts, 11 to air escorts.
By the 24th May, Karl Dönitz had accepted defeat. His U-boats were
withdrawn from the North Atlantic convoy routes.

From June 1943 onwards, merchant ships were being built in
Allied shipyards at a rate much in excess of the losses from all causes,
while U-boats led a harried and haunted existence wherever they
operated. Support Groups of escort ships and 'Hunter-Killer'
Groups, mostly American, each comprising an aircraft-carrier and
a screen of destroyers and operating in support of convoys, took
such a toll that it became rare for a U-boat to survive more than two
patrols.

Contemplating the failure of his hopes, Dönitz says,

> Again and again we debated most earnestly whether a continuation
> of the U-boat campaign was justified in the face of these heavy losses,
> or whether recourse would have to be made to some other means. But
> in view of the vast enemy forces which our U-boats were tying down,
> we came again and again to the same conclusion: 'The U-boat cam-
> paign must be continued with the forces available. Losses, which bear
> no relation to the success achieved, must be accepted, bitter though
> they are.'

Though German submarines were to carry on the war against
Allied shipping to the last day and hour of the war in other parts of

the oceans, never again were they seriously to threaten the vital life-line between Europe and America. Armed with the acoustic homing torpedo they were to return briefly to the North Atlantic, only to be soundly beaten once again. Fitted with the 'schnorkel' breathing tube which enabled them to recharge their batteries while remaining submerged, they tried to regain in inshore waters the initiative they had lost in the ocean spaces. They failed.

The 24th May, 1943, therefore, marks the day on which the Battle of the Atlantic was won, a complete and decisive victory. To quote from Captain Roskill's Official History.

> After forty-five months of unceasing battle of a more exacting and arduous nature than posterity may easily realise, our convoy escorts had won the triumph they so richly merited.

Appendix

Weapons of the Battle of the Atlantic

The Asdic

The asdic was the name by which the sonar device for the detection of a submerged submarine was known. In its first primitive form it was produced towards the end of the First World War by the labours of the Allied Submarine Detection Committee, from whose initials it took its name. Basically it consisted of a transmitter-receiver, which sent out impulses of a sound wave on any selected bearing and picked up the same impulses when they struck an object and were reflected. These transmissions and their echoes were made audible, through earphones or loudspeakers, as a musical note best described as 'Ping'. By mounting the transmitter-receiver so that it could be trained round like a submarine searchlight, the direction in which the 'ping' went out (and consequently the direction in which lay the object from which the 'ping' was reflected) could be read off from a compass receiver. By noting the interval of time between the transmission and the return of its 'echo', the range of the object could be obtained.

So far the theory was quite simple, but in practice a number of circumstances arose to complicate the picture. The transmitter-receiver had obviously to be below the surface of the water, and immersed in the water, and, being by its nature a form of hydrophone, as the ship moved through the water the noise of the water sweeping across it would drown the noise of the 'ping' unless steps were taken to avoid this. So the instrument was encased in a metal 'dome' projecting from the ship's bottom. The dome was filled with water and thus as the ship went ahead the instrument remained immersed in sea-water but relatively stationary sea-water. But even so, only at moderate speeds could the noise level in the asdic be kept low enough for it to function. Therefore, whenever a ship wished to operate its asdic to search for or hunt a submarine it had to moderate its speed.

When searching with the asdic, the procedure was to sweep across a broad arc from one side of the ship's course to the other, stopping every few degrees to transmit a 'ping', listen for any echo coming back, and then to train the asdic round a few degrees and repeat the process. A fairly wide section of water was thus covered by each complete sweep. If several ships were searching together, they would be spread in a line abreast a mile or a mile and a half apart, so that the path swept by the asdic of one ship would be touching the path swept by the ships adjacent, leaving no water unswept between.

Should an echo be received, the sound beam would be held on to it, the range and bearing could be read off and passed to the plotting table and, when a number of such ranges and bearings had been received, the plot operator could read the course and speed of the target. If it was moving at all it might be a U-boat, but, as whales, and shoals of fish also sent back an echo, this was by no means a certainty. Similarly, if stationary, it was unlikely to be a submarine as a submarine generally requires some forward motion to allow its hydroplanes to help it keep at a set depth. On the other hand in shallow water the stationary echo might come from a 'bottomed' submarine.

Thus there were a number of modifications to the simple theoretical operation of the asdic. To an inexperienced operator all echoes were the same: submarines, fish, tide rips, rocks or even sheer imagination. The experienced U-boat hunter, on the other hand, developed a sort of sixth sense. The echo from a submarine was to him in some indefinable and unexplainable way different from any other. But no operator was infallible and always, when sweeping for submarines with the asdic, the decision whether to attack or ignore a contact had to be made. The number of depth-charges available and the desirability of conserving them for more positive contacts, the gap left in the screen by dropping out to attack, the confusion and alarm that might be unnecessarily caused in the convoy if a contact other than a submarine were attacked—all these factors had to be weighed before the decision could be taken.

Once it was decided to attack, the procedure was to point the ship at the target and close it at a moderate speed. By the time the range was down to about 1,000 yards, sufficient data would have reached the plot to give a course and speed of the target. Course would then be altered so as to 'collide' with the submarine, and as the ship passed over it, or rather passed a little way ahead to allow for the time taken by depth-charges to sink, a pattern of depth-charges would be fired. Those from the chutes in the stern would be dropped at evenly spaced intervals in the wake, while the depth-charge throwers would send others out some 50 yards on either side. Thus the pattern properly laid would form a shape like an elongated diamond, somewhere inside of which, it was hoped, would be the target. But to produce lethal damage the charges had to be exploded near the U-boat in depth as well as in plan. A weakness of the asdic, as fitted during the Battle of the Atlantic, was that the target's depth could only be estimated. This was done by taking advantage of an otherwise unfortunate characteristic of the asdic—the fact that contact could not be held down to very short ranges.

The sound beam sent out was conical in shape so that, the farther the impulse travelled, the broader and deeper was the area it covered. Thus, though an object at a depth of, say, 500 feet would be in the beam at a range of 1,000 yards, as the range lessened the object would become below the lower limit of the cone of sound and would thus cease to send back a reflection or echo. This meant that, when running in to deliver a depth-charge attack, there would be a period before firing, varying according to the depth of the target, during which contact would be lost. If the submarine was very deep this might be as long as two minutes, enough for a submarine to make an undetected alteration of course which would take it out of lethal range of the depth-charge pattern.

On the other hand, the range at which contact was lost enabled an estimate of the target's depth to be made. The depth-charge settings controlling the depth at which they would explode could thus be adjusted as necessary. The estimate was only a rough one, however, so that, in combination with the need to forecast the target's movement during the 'dead time' when contact was lost, the destruction of a deep submarine required a considerable element of luck. The enemy soon realised this and many U-boats escaped destruction by going down to the safe diving limit and staying there. It was not until after the period covered by this book that modifications were made to the asdic which enabled the target's depth to be accurately discovered and contact to be held down to the moment of firing.

The Hedgehog

The necessity to pass right over a submerged submarine to attack it with depth-charges and the inability to hold contact up to the moment of firing was a grave handicap in this form of attack. It would obviously be an advantage to be able to stand off and bombard the target. Experiments were therefore started in 1942 to produce the necessary weapon. Two types were designed. A mortar which would throw a pattern of depth-charges and a projector which could do the same with 24 small, contact-fused bombs, to a range of 250 yards.

The former did not reach perfection and go to sea until after the period covered by this book. The latter began to be fitted early in 1943. Known as the Hedgehog, it achieved a number of successes. Its advantage over the depth-charge was that the submarine commander had no warning of attack and so was unable to judge the moment to dodge. Another characteristic was that the bombs, being contact-fused, only exploded if a direct hit was scored. Thus, though an explosion signalled certain destruction of the submarine, a near miss did no damage at all, whereas under depth-charge attack damage sufficient to destroy or to force the submarine to surface could accumulate from a succession of non-lethal near misses.

High Frequency Direction Finder (H/F D/F)

The ability to determine from a ship the direction of a station transmitting on the medium radio frequencies had existed for many years before the war. High frequency (short-wave) transmissions posed special problems however. Their direction could be determined by stations on shore fairly easily, but it was not until the war had been under way for more than two years that an effective direction-finding set for ships was produced.

This, of course, gave only a bearing and not a range, so that to pin-point a transmitting station two or more ships fitted with it and stationed some way apart were needed, the point of intersection of the bearings each obtained giving the position. On the other hand, a distinction could be made by an experienced operator between signals received directly, on the ground wave as it was called, or indirectly, after reflection back to earth from the ionisphere. Ground wave reception was possible only over a short range, 15 to 20 miles from a submarine according to the height of the receiver's aerial. Thus, if a signal was received on the ground wave, it indicated a U-boat close to the receiving ship and probably in contact. The system of control exercised by U-boat Command required frequent signals to be made by the submarines and especially a report whenever contact with a convoy was made. The interception of this by the H/F D/F of an escort thus gave instant warning that the convoy was being shadowed and a rough estimate of the shadower's position.

Next to 10-centimetre radar, H/F D/F comprised the most important element in the winning of the Battle of the Atlantic. In combination with radar it eventually made submarine attack on convoys too hazardous to be attempted.

German torpedoes

German U-boats were equipped at the beginning of the war with air-driven torpedoes similar to British types. These proved not only unreliable in themselves, particularly with regard to depth-keeping, but had warheads fitted with magnetically operated firing devices which also proved ineffective. 'I do not believe', commented Admiral Dönitz, when he read his U-boat commanders' reports on these weapons, 'that ever in the history of war have men been sent against the enemy with such a useless weapon.'

The electric torpedo which was produced to replace this type was all that could be desired. Fitted with a reliable, contact-fired warhead, it was trackless, so that on its explosion there was no indication of the position from which it had been launched. This was the weapon primarily used by German U-boats during the Battle of the Atlantic. Subsequently, they were also armed with a proportion of acoustic 'homing' torpedoes, which were automatically drawn towards the sounds emitted by a ship's propellers. These were designed to hit back at a hunting warship. Even later a torpedo known as a 'Lut' came into use which would steer a pre-determined zig-zag course after a certain length of straight run.

Index

The numerals in bold type denote the *figure* numbers of illustrations